The Cultivated Gardener

A TWO-YEAR GARDEN
JOURNAL

by
Cathy Wilkinson Barash
and
Jim Wilson

photographs by
Cathy Wilkinson Barash

SIMON & SCHUSTER

SIMON & SCHUSTER
Rockefeller Center
1230 Avenue of the Americas
New York, New York 10020

Design by Kathy Klingaman
Design assistant: Nancy A. Judd
Photographs © 1996 Cathy Wilkinson Barash
Printed in Korea

1 3 5 7 9 10 8 6 4 2

ISBN 0-684-80325-9

TABLE OF CONTENTS

JANUARY
Lightening the Load—Lowering Garden Maintenance

FEBRUARY
Fragrance—The Aromatic Garden

MARCH
Beautiful Food—Using Fruits, Vegetables, and Herbs in the Landscape

APRIL
Controlling Wildlife in the Garden

MAY
Color and Texture for Contrast

JUNE
Vertical Gardens—Growing Up

JULY
Edible Flowers for Beauty and Flavor

AUGUST
Evening Gardens—Gardens for Evening Enjoyment

SEPTEMBER
Shade—An Asset in the Landscape

OCTOBER
Water Gardens

NOVEMBER
Variegation—Plants of Distinction

DECEMBER
Sounds from the Garden

APPENDIX
Charts of Plants

INTRODUCTION

By definition, a journal can be a personal record of experiences or reflections, in other words, a diary. As such, it would be a blank book, ready for your entries. This journal is a memory jogger, a gardener's almanac of gardening duties and opportunities that you have forgotten—or may have not lived long enough to learn.

The great cycle of seasons is something we all know and think we understand. But the effect of the seasons on each person's garden and on individual plants is less easily comprehended. It is an ongoing process of observing and relating cause and effect that doesn't cease until the final day of a gardener's life.

The goings and comings of the seasons are beyond our control, so other than praising or complaining about them, we take them for granted. We understand that the relative tilt of the earth on its axis regulates that seemingly eternal cycle and that the seasons are the major determinant of regional climates. And after living in one place for several years we begin to understand how large bodies of water, mountains, prevailing winds and exposure to them, air drainage, fog, and urban warmth can create microclimates within local areas.

But not until we have gardened on one piece of land for many years do we understand that a single piece of property may have even smaller microclimates within its boundaries, created by sun and shade, exposure to wind, windbreaks of trees or fences, wind tunnels between buildings, the tilt or slope of the land toward or away from the sun, and light and heat reflected or radiated from walls. That understanding comes from observing the reactions of plants in our own and other landscapes, by opening all our senses and looking up, down, and all around rather than right at the plant.

Experienced gardeners waste little time or effort on unadapted plants. Instead, they concentrate on making the best use of the growing season ordained by their climate. Some, in short season areas, use shelters of various sorts to extend the growing season fore and aft. Wherever they garden, they know not to assume that any new plant, product, or process will succeed in their garden,

that all have to be tried under their growing conditions and o their soil. They aren't being cynical, just practical. For these reasons, the regional recommendations within thi journal must of necessity be general. We could have used th numbered regions of the USDA Hardiness Zone Map to identi our regions, but chose not to because the USDA zones were determined mostly by minimum winter temperatures. The map's hardiness zones extend from northern Canada down into Mexico. Instead, we elected to use only five very gener zones and to identify them by letters to avoid confusio

Regions A through E

Region A Far north, upper Great Plains, and high-altitude areas

Region B Lower Great Lakes, central Great Plains, New England, and the cold valleys east of the Cascades

Region C The broad belt across the middle of the country, the lower Great Plains, and intermountain valleys with warm summers

Region D Upper and Middle South, middle elevations of the Southwest and northern California, and valleys west of the Cascades

Region E Central and southern Florida; a sheltered belt along the Gulf Coast, far south Texas, southern California, and low elevations of the Southwest

Note: Gardeners in Alaska and Hawaii have unique climates and microclimates that are too special to be covered in a journal of general information.

As you progress in gardening you will learn that hardly anything is exact and predictable, especially wh it applies to climates and devices for categorizing them For example, southerners and gardeners in hot areas o the West know that the USDA Hardiness Zone Map do not measure the ability of a plant to survive their summers. Eventually, a supplement may be issued that doe just that.

Certain regional publications such as *Sunset* magazine publish highly detailed maps, with zones based o years of notations on coastal or inland weather, and ele vations of valleys and mountainside sites. In the West, the *Sunset* climate zone map is considered more accura than the USDA map, and its ratings of plant adaptabili consider summer highs as well as winter lows.

How to Use this Journal

No journal can cover all the things a gardener needs to do in all climates. You are encouraged to read not only the points that apply to your region for a particular month, but also information for other regions and other months. Add the information to your memory bank; you may be able to convert it to fit your garden. At the least, it can help you to understand the challenges of gardeners in other regions as you travel around.

Treat this journal as a catalyst. Don't limit your reading to just the month at hand, nor allow a single reading of this journal to suffice. Get a pad of little paste-on notes and jot down the thoughts generated by the monthly reminders. Stick them in the book. After a few passes through the journal, you can begin compiling your personal calendar/journal. Take it with you as you visit other private, botanical, or estate gardens, and continue to jot down your observations on plant cultivars, culture, and landscaping details. You will find that your own calendar/journal plus permanent plant labels in your own garden will become your two most important allies in improving your gardening skills.

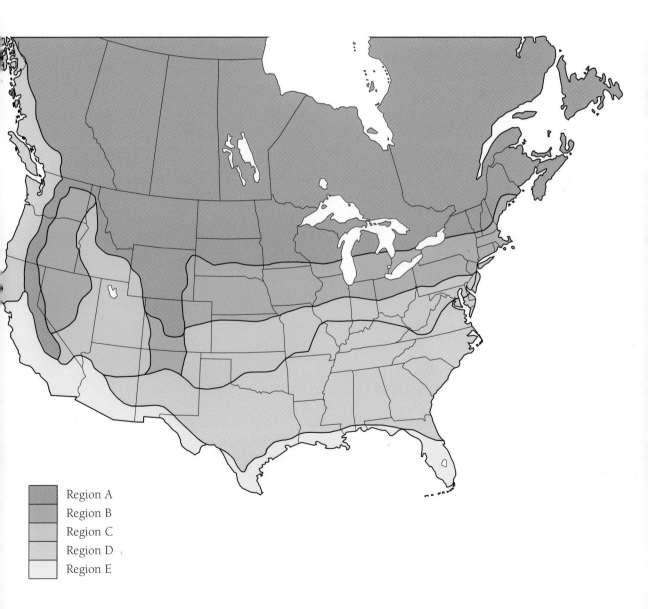

Region A
Region B
Region C
Region D
Region E

JANUARY

Lightening the Load— Lowering Garden Maintenance

No matter how large or small your garden is, there never seems to be enough time to do the garden chores and have time left to simply enjoy the garden. Much has been written in the past decade about low-maintenance gardening. While talking to gardeners (and those who consider themselves nongardeners, yet are homeowners who grow plants or keep up their property), I learned that the term "low maintenance" is truly subjective. To some it means a garden that requires only an hour or two of work once a week; to others it means a garden that requires little or no watering and/or weeding. Then there are those who have large properties, to whom a low-maintenance garden is one that a single, full-time gardener can maintain, rather than a crew of three or more. Whatever your definition of low maintenance is, you will find suggestions here to lighten the load in your garden.

One of the most important considerations for a low-maintenance garden is choosing the right plant for the location. Educate yourself about your garden space. Make a rough drawing of your property, and then observe it. Write down how many hours of sun a day each planting area gets. Know the soil type and pH. Note which areas are sheltered and which areas may be affected by winds.

Try not to be seduced into buying the gorgeous plant in perfect bloom at the garden center, or those pictured in the plant catalogues, without checking that the plant is indeed suitable for your garden. If it is, by all means buy it. If not, you can probably grow it in a container according to its special needs. In the garden, always remember the old adage, "Plant a 50-cent plant in a $5 hole." Dig a hole at least twice as wide and deep as the root ball. Check the drainage, digging deeper and adding plenty of organic material if the hole does not drain well. Amend the soil from the hole with rich organic material (compost, leaf mulch, or peat moss).

Adjust the pH level if necessary. Backfill the hole halfway with amended soil, then set your plant in place. Fill in with the rest of the soil. Water well.

The single most-timesaving device for any gardener is using mulch around the plants. Mulches perform several functions. A layer of mulch several inches thick provides a barrier to weeds; most weed seeds in the ground do not have enough light and air to grow through the mulch, and the ground is protected against potential weed seeds dropped by birds or animals. An organic mulch (such as chopped leaves, pine needles, leaf mold, or shredded bark) conserves water; it stays moist, keeping the ground from drying, especially in the heat of summer. Use an organic mulch and you get a bonus: as the mulch decomposes, nutrients are added to the soil. A mulch of gravel or small stones is a good choice around plants that like to be dry. The choice of mulch and the time of year you apply it affects the soil temperature. In general, a light-colored mulch reflects light and heat toward the plant, while a dark mulch absorbs heat to the soil level. A layer of black plastic applied in late winter or early spring warms the soil, especially on a raised bed, to give you a jump start on planting. Apply a winter mulch too early in the fall, while the ground is still warm, and you insulate the soil, keeping it warm. Instead, wait until the ground is cold or frozen to mulch, and that thick layer will help prevent heaving of the soil as temperatures rise above and below freezing.

Many watering practices waste both time and water. The best way to water is right at soil level, where the water can easily seep down into the soil to the roots. You can choose from different types of ground-level systems—do-it-yourself drip irrigation systems, leaky hose, or even hand watering at the base of the plants. Water early in the morning, especially if using a sprinkler. That way, any water that gets on the leaves evaporates; constantly wet leaves can lead to mildew or fungal disease. When you water, water slowly and deeply, so that the top 3 to 4 inches of soil are moistened. This way plants are encouraged to grow deeper roots, and you will need to water less often.

Raised beds are another time and energy saver. The simplest raised bed is one built up 6 to 10 inches above ground level by raking or shoveling soil onto the bed from adjacent areas. For those with physical limitations, and especially those of us with bad backs, an enclosed bed, up to 3 feet tall, makes gardening chores a breeze. Any type of raised bed has the advantage of warming up earlier in the spring, and it has better drainage and easier access to plants than beds at ground level. You will find that plants get off to a better start because they can spread their roots deeper than in most unimproved soils.

Previous page: *Pine needle mulch with pansies and iris*

Except in the semitropical or Mediterranean-climate gardens of Region E, and occasional balmy days in Region D, involvement with your garden has to be mostly through your imagination and through memories of gardens past. January days are too cold to venture out except to recharge the bird feeders and to set out shallow containers of water. Resolve to keep a garden journal... and add photographs or a video record. Take your journal with you once a week on a stroll through your garden. Record the date and the names of plants that are in bloom or peak production and your observations on needed additions or changes. The following winter, plan improvements and changes as a remedy for restlessness or cabin fever.

Regions A, B, C, D, E Plan your new garden; order seeds, plants, and supplies.

Regions A, B, C, D Shear the limbs off Christmas trees—lay them over dwarf conifers to minimize winter damage.

Regions C, D, E If water stands anywhere in your garden, cut a ditch to let it drain. If the problem is serious and long-standing, consider having a contractor run a "mole" from the wet spot to a lower area and insert a drainpipe. Cover the outlet and inlet with screen to keep out small animals and trash.

Regions B, C, D Should you have dry weather for two weeks or more, water well. Your broad-leaved evergreens, especially, can suffer from winter drought. More plants die from desiccation than from extreme cold.

Regions B, C, D Lay in supplies for growing plants outdoors in containers—vegetables and herbs as well as flowers.

Pot shards make an attractive mulch

HINTS, CLUES, AND ADVICE

↶ Keep mulch ½ to 1" away from the stems of plants and trees. Mulching too closely may suffocate or bruise tender plants. Mulch placed too close to a tree trunk can encourage insect damage or rot.

↶ Consider the color of the plants and flowers, especially if low to the ground, when choosing a mulch. Very dark flowers show up better on a light mulch. Be wary of sawdust or homemade wood chips. Their gray or yellowish cast can be an unattractive background with many plants.

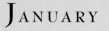

Regions A, B, C, D, E Build or repair bluebird and wren boxes.

Regions A, B, C, D Don't walk on frozen lawns—grass in frost-heaved soil is fragile.

Regions A, B, C, D Shake or sweep snow off your conifers and broad-leaved evergreens. Protect yews from windburn with a burlap fence.

Regions B, C, D, E Turn the compost heap. Have a cat or terrier nearby to dispatch evicted mice.

Regions B, C, D Prune fruit trees and grape vines. Don't cut off branches flush with the trunk—leave a half-inch collar to promote rapid healing. Ask your Cooperative Extension Service for bulletins on how to prune the various trees and vines.

Regions B, C, D Prune roses, except for climbers and related pillar roses that bloom on old canes; trim them just enough to keep them neat.

Regions C, D Pull out and compost last year's annuals; the birds will have gleaned all the seeds by now.

Region E Feed houseplants, especially large tropicals. Set them on the patio on a warm day and pour clear water through them until it runs out the bottom, then pour liquid plant food over the soil. Repeat every 7 to 10 days.

Companion planting—daffodils, tulips, hyacinths

HINTS, CLUES, AND ADVICE

↶ Go out and look closely at your plants at least once a week. At the first sign of insects or disease, treat the individual plant. Try to figure out what made it a target for predation. Are you watering too much or too little? Consider moving the plant to a more suitable location.

Regions A, B, C, D, E Clean out and refill bird feeders weekly. Be sure to provide water—best done in shallow plastic containers.

Regions A, B, C, D, E Inspect the stems and leaf undersides of houseplants frequently for insects such as mealybugs, cottony-cushion scale, and spider mites. Dab stems with a cotton-tipped swab dipped in rubbing alcohol; spray beneath leaves with insecticidal soap every two days for a week to kill mites. Try the new biological insecticides based on the oil of the neem tree.

Regions A, B, C Order narcissus and amaryllis bulbs for forcing.

Regions C, D On the occasional warm day, check perennials to be sure that mulch has not been blown or washed too deeply over the crowns.

Regions B, C, D, E Repot winter-weary houseplants. If they are severely potbound, snip the girdling roots and shift the plant to the next-larger-size pot.

Regions B, C, D Toward the end of the month apply preemergence herbicides to keep crabgrass and other weeds from sprouting in your lawn. If you object to herbicides and manufactured fertilizers, use an organic lawn food sans herbicide. More and more gardeners are developing a tolerant attitude toward broad-leaved plants growing among lawn grass.

Region E If the tip growth of citrus, fig, or hibiscus trees has turned yellow, suspect iron deficiency—correct it with chelated iron or a micronutrient blend, applied every time you water, until symptoms disappear.

Raised beds

HINTS, CLUES, AND ADVICE

~ Get your soil pH tested every two years. Your local Cooperative Extension Service can perform the tests for a minimal fee, and will advise you how to properly collect the samples. Take samples from different areas around your property, making sure to label them so you know the location.

Regions A, B, C, D, E Provide a wildlife habitat on your home grounds. Begin with wildflowers, trees, and shrubs native to your region. Your local library is a good source of information on plant species good for feeding and sheltering hummingbirds, butterflies, and songbirds.

Regions A, B, C, D, E Set houseplants in the shower stall or bathtub, and run tepid water through the soil to leach out accumulated salts. Reduce watering frequency and don't feed plants during midwinter. Don't water or feed cacti or related euphorbias until the days grow longer and brighter.

Regions A, B, C, D, E Fill saucers, plates, or aluminum pie pans with pebbles to set beneath houseplant pots; keep the saucers filled halfway with water to increase humidity.

Regions C, D, E Start quick-growing seeds under lights: sweet basil, marigolds, zinnias, and tomatoes.

Regions B, C, D Remove old berry canes at the base—check the mulch around strawberries; replace it where thin.

Regions B, C, D Watch for the occasional warm day when the soil is dry enough to work. Mix sharp sand or granite meal and finely pulverized pine bark into heavy soils to make raised beds—use organic matter alone on sandy soils. On acidic soils in the South, apply lime; it is rarely needed in the West and Southwest.

Region E Set out cold-tolerant annuals and perennials: fragrant stock, calendula, primula, calceolaria, nemesia, and schizanthus. If frost is forecast, protect plants with floating row covers held down with bricks.

TIP OF THE MONTH:

Paint wooden handles of garden tools a bright color—not only to prevent them from weathering and cracking but also to help you find them quickly. Happiness is seeing a rake or hoe rather than stepping on it. Some of the new garden tools come with tough, slick, brightly colored plastic sheathing around the wooden core or virtually unbreakable enameled steel handles.

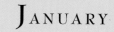

Straw mulch with drip irrigation

HINTS, CLUES, AND ADVICE

～ Use the space in your garden to its optimum potential. Interplant perennials with early-flowering bulbs. The perennial's leaves hide the yellowing foliage of the bulbs, allowing the bulbs to store as much energy from the leaves as possible for their dormant period.

FEBRUARY

Fragrance—
The Aromatic Garden

Nothing is quite so wonderful as to walk outside and be enveloped in the delightful aromas emanating from the garden. Ancient pleasure gardens were punctuated with sweetly fragrant plants to exemplify the romantic aspect of the garden.

Although you may think of fragrance in the garden as a warm-weather, daytime phenomenon, scented plants span the four seasons. Many plants exude their fragrance at night. We may enjoy the sweet aroma, but the smell is actually intended to lure their pollinators.

Smell is perhaps the most subjective of all the senses. The ability to perceive smell is highly variable, not only from person to person, but within yourself. You know that when you have a cold, you cannot smell anything. I can pick up sweet aromas from flowers that others cannot, so I enjoy more of the garden for its fragrance. However, too much of anything is not necessarily good. A friend has such a keen sense of smell that he is easily sensorially overloaded by many garden plants.

Consider how great the range of smells is in the plant world. There is the sweet perfume from a rose, the honey-like scent of a winter aconite, the light floral note of a sweet violet, the heady sweetness of a gardenia, the richly intoxicating aroma of a moonflower, the citrus essence of an orange tree in bloom, and the delightful scent of a lilac. You may find some smells, like marigolds, appealing, while to others the scent is somewhat rank. Some flowers and plants have unpleasant scents. Skunk cabbage, attractive in a bog garden, would not be welcome outside the bedroom window.

Don't look to just the flowers for fragrance—the leaves of some plants are aromatic. To give off their aroma, the leaves of these plants often need to be slightly bruised or crushed. Plant them at the edge of a path, or use small plants between stepping-stones so that they can easily be brushed against or touched. Among the best plants for leaf aromas are the wide range of herbs. I plant a rose-scented geranium near the front door, so I can just brush my hand on a leaf and enjoy the light rose essence for hours. Consider the possibilities: perfumed lavender, licorice-scented anise hyssop, spicy-minty bee balm, cool cucumbery borage, apple-scented chamomile, oniony chives and garlic chives, medicinal hyssop, aromatic sage or rosemary, hay-like sweet woodruff, or the sharp pungency of rue. The many varieties of Eucalyptus or gum tree have a wide range of smells to their leaves, from honey-like to pungent, pepperminty to camphoraceous.

Too many scented plants set closely together can be off-putting. I like to allow at least 10 to 15 feet between strongly scented plants. Or choose plants that bloom at different times of year. In a 3x12-foot section of my garden, the aromatic year begins in late January with Chinese witch hazel. A 6-inch branch of witch hazel with its small yellow, ribbon-like flowers can perfume my bathroom for a week. Soon, at the base of the shrub, dainty snowdrops appear with their nodding white heads smelling cool and mossy. I like to have a miniature bouquet of them on my night table. Crocuses are scattered throughout the garden bed, giving off a scent of honey on a warm spring day. Sweetly scented daffodils follow, grouped in clumps of seven or nine bulbs. Before long, the chamomile, which self-seeds, begins to sprout, sending up its ferny, apple-scented foliage. Interspersed in the spring garden are pansies and English daisies—pretty and not fragrant. A few heady hyacinths complete the spring garden. As summer approaches, daylily foliage hides the withering bulbs. 'Citron' is fragrant, opening in late afternoon. Summer hyacinths, perfume the air, while other summer-blooming annuals and perennials dazzle the eye. At the other end of the bed, a stand of old-fashioned flowering tobacco is fronted with a new pink hybrid. The old-fashioned ones come into their own at night, attracting sphinx moths and other pollinators with their sweet smell. The new hybrids are barely fragrant, but act as an attractive screen for the gawky foliage of the old-fashioned variety. Fragrant double tuberoses and cheery chrysanthemums interplanted with ornamental kale finish out the gardening season in fall.

When I started consciously adding fragrance to the garden, I went a bit overboard. Near the bedroom window were moonflowers, summer hyacinths, tuberoses, nicotiana, and stock. Although some of these don't normally bloom at the same time, they all were in profusion at once. When the evenings were breezy, we enjoyed sitting outside—a distance from the plants. On a still, hot night, the cloyingly strong and clashing fragrance from all the blooms was overpowering.

Previous page: *Rubrum lilies*

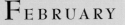

The days grow longer during February, but not rapidly enough to stop the flight of "snowbirds" to southern climes. Spring is well under way in Florida, the Southwest, low elevations in California, and along the Gulf Coast, while the North is still locked in the grip of winter. If you can't afford to flee the cold, or prefer not to buck the crowds heading for resorts, consider installing a propagation and growing area for plants in your basement or in a spare room. The most important requirement for an indoor growing area is that it can be kept on the cool side, 60 to 65 degrees F. during the day, and 55 to 60 degrees at night.

Regions A, B, C, D, E Hang suet in wire mesh containers to foil cats and rodents. Insect-eating birds need the fat. When planning a backyard wildlife habitat, be sure to include dense berry-bearing shrubs that provide shelter and nesting sites for birds, as well as winter food.

Regions D, E Plant tree peonies for drama. They have enormous blossoms with a silken sheen. Give them afternoon shade and adequate moisture to ensure a good set of flower buds and to prolong the short life of individual blossoms.

Region E Set out pepper, eggplant, melon, sweet potato, and tomato plants, but protect from frost with floating row covers.

Above: *Scented geranium*, Pelargonium sp.

HINTS, CLUES AND, ADVICE

⌣ Plant lemon thyme between stepping-stones or brick pavers for a light fresh scent. The thyme is too fragile to step on it continually, but the occasional grazing of a foot releases its lemony fragrance into the air.

Regions A, B, C, D, E When starting seeds indoors, use a near-sterile mixture of peat moss and vermiculite. Most garden centers sell special seed-starting mixes.

Regions A, B, C Clean indoor plants heavily infested with mealy bugs by fitting a cardboard collar over the container to hold soil in place. Invert the plant and immerse it in a bucket or tub of mild insecticidal soap solution. Repeat two or three times every few days if necessary.

Region D Mid-February is a good time to divide perennials in the South. If plants have not been doing well in full sun, set the divisions where they will get afternoon shade.

Region D Pecan trees are a major yard tree across the humid South. Now is the time to feed them and to spread lime to counteract soil acidity. Don't concentrate the fertilizer and lime beneath the foliage canopy, but spread it in a wide band outside of the drip line where the feeder roots are concentrated. A large tree can use 40 pounds of low-nitrogen fertilizer every growing season to maintain maximum nut production.

Region E Groom your tropicals. Thin congested plants, remove unsightly leaves stem and all, and give them a good feeding to promote luxuriant growth. Bougainvilleas bloom best if kept slightly potbound in containers or, in soil, fed with low-nitrogen fertilizers.

Saucer magnolia

H I N T S ,   C L U E S ,   A N D   A D V I C E

❧ Limit the number and types of fragrant plants in
your garden. Allow plenty of space between different
plants as their scents, when mixed, may be overpowering.

Regions A, B, C, D, E Overcome short days and low sunlight levels with fluorescent tubes or metal halide lamps. Hang fluorescent lights only 2 inches above the tops of seeded trays, 6 inches above houseplants.

Regions A, B, C If you find that salt has damaged or killed patches of grass bordering walks, rake away the dead plants, scatter a bit of potting soil or garden compost, and broadcast grass seed over it. Try to match the dominant grass species in your lawn to avoid a patchy look.

Region D Prune roses. Paint cut tips to discourage borers from entering. When mild winters come, roses can bloom all winter long, and it seems a shame to cut off wood that could produce buds. If you don't, however, stem diameter and blossom size can diminish.

Region D Yes, you can grow lilacs in the South. The selection of adapted cultivars is limited, and you may have to spray for mildew, but they are worth the trouble. By and large, though, the new mildew-resistant crape myrtles are a better bet.

Region D Fill and hang hummingbird feeders two weeks before the birds' usual arrival. Coat the wire hanger with Vaseline or Vick's Salve to keep ants from climbing down it from the tree or stand.

Region E Feed your lawn. But remember that high-nitrogen urea or ammonium fertilizers can burn if not washed off grass within 5 minutes of application. Make this the year you begin leaving grass clippings where they fall. It means more frequent mowing but your lawn will need less fertilizer and will have fewer problems with thatch.

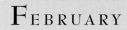

Beach rose, Rosa rugosa

HINTS, CLUES, AND ADVICE

↜ Be cautious when planting highly scented plants near windows of the house. A gardenia planted outside the bedroom window sounds like a lovely idea, but in reality, the scent of many flowers in full bloom can be cloyingly sweet, especially if there is no breeze to dilute the smell.

Regions A, B, C, D, E Sprout cress, alfalfa, or bean seeds under lights for fresh salads. Start them in glass quart jars laid on the side. Soak 2 tablespoons of seeds overnight; add them to jars along with 2 tablespoons of water, and shake gently to distribute them evenly.

Region D If growth on your crinum bulbs is becoming congested, dig and divide them. A 5-year-old bulb will sometimes divide into a dozen bulbs from golf-ball to grapefruit size. Warning: except in loose, sandy soil, digging and dividing an old mother crinum bulb is a huge project.

Region D Interest children in plants. Start a sweet potato or a carrot or pineapple top in water or potting soil, or save and sprout an avocado seed.

Regions D, E If you missed the first flight of purple martins, hang martin gourds or set up martin apartment houses now. Late arrivers may occupy them. Actually, bats are better at consuming the insects that trouble gardens and landscapes. If you have a patch of woods, consider putting up a bat house. (Oh, go ahead and do it! Never mind what the neighbors might say!)

TIP OF THE MONTH:

The longer you garden, the more you become aware that no one can possibly learn everything there is to know about home horticulture. It is an enormous field, spanning everything from plant propagation to soil preparation and improvement, pest identification and control, plant identification, lawn care, and landscape design. This is why most gardeners, sooner or later, specialize in one or more hobby crops that they can learn in depth. If you have an affinity for a certain plant species, begin collecting cultivars of it. But if you remain a "general" gardener, and need basic gardening information, nothing can beat enrolling in a Master Gardening course offered by the Cooperative Extension Service in most states. By all means, buy garden books, but look for titles by North American authors. British garden writers are good, especially in landscape design, but their books often recommend cultivars unavailable in this country or practices inappropriate for our wildly gyrating climates.

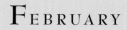

Anise hyssop with cleome

HINTS, CLUES, AND ADVICE

⌒ To add an exotic air to your garden, include some night-blooming or night-fragrant plants. Plant them where you can get their best effect—along a walkway, by the garage (if you come home after dark), or even near your compost pile (assuming you empty the day's kitchen scraps in the evening).

MARCH

Beautiful Food— Using Fruits, Vegetables, & Herbs in the Landscape

One of my first garden memories is of planting tomatoes in the flower bed alongside the marigolds. My outraged father pulled up the tomatoes and replanted them in the vegetable bed where he said they belonged. Many years later I discovered I had been simply creating an edible landscape—which the ancient Egyptians had started centuries before me.

Egyptian pleasure gardens, sometimes enclosed, with fish ponds, beautiful flowers, grape arbors, and fruiting trees provided a place to sit and enjoy the serenity. By the Renaissance, vegetables and herbs were often put into stylized gardens of their own. Fruit and nut trees were a prized part of the garden until the early part of the twentieth century. Since then, more formal landscaping has thrived, with a focus on ornamental plants. With the heightened ecological awareness in the 1980s, edibles began to be recognized for their dual purposes—beauty and edibility, and they have been reintroduced into the general landscape.

Edibles encompass the entire range of plants: trees (nuts and fruit), shrubs (berries), annuals (most vegetables, herbs, and edible flowers), perennials (some vegetables, herbs, and edible flowers), and even vines (fruits and vegetables). Most are attractive—for their flowers, foliage, fruit, form, or texture—in addition to having one or more edible parts. Landscaping commonly uses sterile hybrids of spring-flowering trees such as pears, cherries, and crabapples; their fruiting cousins are equally attractive when they bloom in spring, with the bonus of free, handsome, and delicious fruit in summer or fall.

It is unlikely you will redo your entire landscape with edibles, nor is that necessary. Instead, simply consider using an edible whenever you are adding to your landscape. For instance, if a large tree dies or is damaged, think about replacing it with a nut tree suitable for your climate. A full-sized fruit tree might be a good replacement for a medium-sized deciduous ornamental tree. Many fruit trees are now available as genetic dwarfs, making them suitable for foundation plantings or even as containerized plants.

Be certain the chosen site is suitable for the plant. Blueberries are attractive as foundation plants, but they need acidic soil. Blueberries grow well, although they need more sun, in the same acidic soil as azaleas, rhododendrons, mountain laurel, and heather. A fig tree also makes a good foundation plant (in northern climates, shelter it in a south-facing location out of the wind).

Fences provide a good support for training fruit trees. You can plant brambles, such as raspberries, blackberries, or gooseberries tightly to create a living fence. Some of the shrub roses, such as *Rosa rugosa,* produce large, bright orange or red, edible rose hips in late summer or fall. The fruit has 60 times the vitamin C of an orange and can be used to make tea or, more commonly, jam and jelly. Peas are lovely trained on a fence and can be followed by cucumbers or squash as the season progresses.

An arbor or trellis is a good addition to an edible landscape. Grapes are commonly trained on arbors, and hardy kiwi, perfect for a large arbor, can grow to 10 feet high. Scarlet runner beans are handsome on an arbor or trellis, with their delicious beans and bright red-orange flowers. Train indeterminate tomato varieties on a trellis or arbor; let the side shoots grow in for maximum coverage.

Perennial herbs can be the backbone of an edible border. Lavender and rosemary have upright forms with thin leaves, providing interest even the winter. Thyme and oregano are low growing and prostrate, best suited for the edge of the garden. Plant them between stepping-stones, where they may be lightly stepped on, releasing their fragrance, or stick them in crevices and nooks in rock or brick walls.

Whatever you do to make your garden a more edible landscape, you cannot help but reap the rewards of your labor.

Previous page: *Grape arbor*

Spring travels like a great circus parade from the tropics to the arctic regions. While the advance publicists may just be putting up posters in the far north, the lions, tigers, and elephants are passing through Mid-America, and the steam calliope, trailed by mobs of children, is bringing up the rear along Southern and Southwestern streets ablaze with flowers. It's okay if you stand up and cheer when spring comes, even to break into song; it's as if the whole wide earth were reborn.

Regions A, B, C, D, E Plan to plant special flowers to attract and feed hummingbirds, butterflies, and seed-eating songbirds. Your library will have books on butterfly and hummingbird gardens.

Regions A, B There's still time to order seeds for indoor starting, but don't delay. The longer you wait, the greater the chance of the most popular kinds being sold out.

Regions A, B Cut and force branches of forsythia, flowering quince, and pussy willows.

Regions C, D, E, Consider putting up window boxes for planting colorful annuals. Boxes should be at least one foot deep and one foot front to back. In the Deep South, mount boxes beneath east or north-facing windows.

Region D Cypress vine, a native American, scarlet-flowered, sun-loving annual, grows quickly from seeds and attracts hummingbirds. But for woodland plantings, consider woody native vines such as cross vine and Carolina jasmine.

Region E Dress up your yard with groups of containers planted with heat-resistant flowers and trailing vines. Use containers that hold at least 5 gallons to reduce the frequency of watering. Fill them with porous "nursery mixes" of pine bark and peat moss.

Parsley, dahlias, and anise hyssop with beeskeep

HINTS, CLUES, AND ADVICE

~ Research before you plant. Go to the grocery store and note which vegetables and fruits are your favorites, paying special attention to the prices. It might be better to use limited space for raspberries, costing more than $3 a pint, than for zucchini, which can be less than 20 cents a pound in season. Asparagus is never cheap; its season is short, and its fern-like foliage is attractive in the summer garden after the harvest is over.

Regions A, B, C Hold off on feeding houseplants, and water infrequently. When days are short and gray, plants grow too slowly to take up many nutrients or much water.

Regions B, C Wait for a tolerably warm day to prune your fruit trees and grape vines; don't risk frostbite. While out, apply a dormant oil spray for overwintering insects and peach leaf curl.

Region B Replace any old, disease-prone lilac cultivars with showier and more disease-resistant cultivars.

Region C Divide and reset chrysanthemum plants before the sprouts begin to lengthen. If you are tired of some colors, order some of the new "Prophet" series developed by Yoder Brothers.

Regions C, D Like bamboo but afraid of its spreading? Try the well-behaved clumping type. Canes come in yellow, green, and black.

Regions D, E Order a catalog from a specialist in old roses. Some of the species of roses and rugged hybrids have considerable resistance to black spot and mildew.

Region E Replace dead tropicals with new plants. Remember to set them well away from the house; they grow fast and can block windows.

Tomatoes trained on an A-frame

HINTS, CLUES, AND ADVICE

➝ While nut and fruit trees may be good investments for the future, be aware that, depending on the variety and size when planted, they may not produce nuts or fruit for many years. Given the choice, it is often worth spending the extra money to buy the largest plant so that you can begin harvesting within a year or two.

➝ Plant some herbs, salad greens, and a tomato in containers near your kitchen door. Easy accessibility means that you are likely to open the door and pick them for immediate use, no matter what the weather— very hot or rainy. You will find your yields on these plants very high, as you will keep picking, encouraging new leaf and fruit formation.

Regions A, B, C When sawing off lower limbs of shade trees to admit more light to flower beds, undercut first to prevent the heavy branch from tearing off a strip of bark from the trunk as it drops. Note: don't "limb up" conifers.

Region B, C Steel yourself to clean the house sparrows out of bluebird nests. Do it during a warm spell, when birds are not huddled inside to keep warm. Spray or dust the interior of the bird house to kill mites, but use a quick-decaying insecticide that won't harm birds with a residue.

Regions A, B, C Still growing the washed-out old iris from Grandma's garden? Replace them with the incredible new colors and graceful blossom forms available in new cultivars.

Region D If you live in a low-elevation area of California or the Southwest and are concerned about expensive water bills, consider mulching some areas with stone and reducing turf to small spots, mostly for green relief. "Xeriscaping" is the term used for landscaping that requires minimum water; xeriscapes can be quite beautiful, if not as lush as water-hungry, inappropriate Eastern planting styles. Native trees, shrubs, and herbaceous plants make up much of the planting palette for xeriscapes.

Region E Ask your garden center for some of the new salvia cultivars for all-summer color.

Variagated sages

HINTS, CLUES, AND ADVICE

✑ For a sunny hillside, consider growing winter squash and pumpkins. The vigorous vines keep the soil from eroding, without bullying other plants. The dark green leaves are attractive, and the variety of shapes and colors of the squash and pumpkins provide interest throughout the autumn.

✑ In a moist, boggy area you can grow the best celery you will ever eat. Watercress flourishes in a small stream.

Regions A, B, C   Contact a certified and licensed arborist for top-working your shade trees. Such experts know how to trim trees for long-term health. Double-check their insurance, both for their employees and for potential damage to your home.

Regions A, B   If you live in or near a state with natural prairies, you can grow a "prairie garden" of flowering species and grasses found in undisturbed prairies. Start with plants, because the seed-to-first-bloom cycle can take from three to five years. If you start with seeds, order from a prairie seed specialist, and plant the flowering species first. Let them grow for two years, then plug in a few plants of the shorter prairie grasses. Two years later, plug in a few of the taller, more robust prairie grasses, and soon you'll have a pretty good facsimile of a true prairie.

Region C   If the worst of the cold weather is past, prune your roses. Too-early pruning will encourage new growth, that can be killed back by a late freeze.

Regions D, E   Water gardens are more popular in the South and warm West than in the North because weather stresses are fewer. When planning a water garden, go for the largest one you can afford, providing it is in scale with your landscape. Site it in full sun where surface drainage won't dump into it, and where it won't be blown full of leaves in the fall. Design it to look as natural as possible, and follow the installation, curing, planting, and stocking instructions of the pool supplier as closely as possible.

TIP OF THE MONTH:
Beware of ads promising plants or products that seem too good to be true. Every year brings a new garden ripoff, often from the same shady operator doing business under a new name. New gardeners are the most vulnerable, because they don't know how to analyze new plant or product offers for credibility. Most mail-order seed and plant companies are impeccably honest and spend a substantial part of their income in research and development. You will find one that will deliver at the right time for your zone, treat you fairly, and offer plants adapted to your climate. When you do, stick with that one.

Ripe tomatoes in rainbow hues

HINTS, CLUES, AND ADVICE

↝ Rhubarb and asparagus can become the backbone of a small perennial border. In spring, cut and cook the stems of each, freezing some to enjoy in winter. After the harvest, the true beauty of both plants emerges. Asparagus grows tall with fern-like foliage, bearing small red berries in autumn. Rhubarb's handsome red stalks are somewhat hidden by large, poisonous leaves. In summer it sends up a tall stalk of small cream-colored flowers. Later, the dark seed surrounded by a semitransparent covering serves well in dried flower arrangements.

↝ Grow some edibles in containers for convenience and easy accessibility. Dwarf citrus can even be grown indoors in northern climates if kept in a cool, sunny location.

APRIL

E. Wilson

Controlling Wildlife in the Garden

Much has been written about attracting wildlife to the garden in recent years. Yet, depending on the size and scope of your garden, some wildlife may not be so desirable. Insects and animals make up most of the wildlife pests. While some wildlife in the garden is beneficial and entertaining, other creatures can get out of control.

Butterfly gardening is one of the hottest trends in gardening today. What you may not realize is that some of the caterpillars considered garden pests in spring and summer metamorphose into the beautiful butterflies and moths you prize as they flit through the garden gathering nectar. The striped parsleyworm or celeryworm, which voraciously eats parsley, celery, dill, and carrots, eventually turns into the lovely black swallowtail butterfly. Unaware of this transformation, you may unwittingly kill off the potential butterflies by spraying the plants with Bt (Bacillus thuringiensis). Plant a large patch of parsley in another garden plot for the hungry larvae, and if they get out of control in your veggies, handpick and move them to their new feeding ground. Another majestic transformation is the hornworm (host plants include beets, currants, grapes, melon, pears, plums, and tomatoes) that becomes a whitelined sphinx moth—a delicate creature resembling a small hummingbird. The tomato hornworm becomes a five-spotted hawkmoth, and the tobacco hornworm turns into a Carolina sphinx moth.

Some of the peskier wildlife includes our own dogs and cats. They should not dissuade you from planting a garden. Certain modifications may be necessary to create a garden whose beauty you can enjoy, while having a space for the pet. Ideally you can train the pet while it is young to use only certain areas for its toilet. Consider a tough ground cover as an alternative to grass. Pachysandra, ivy, and myrtle are all attractive and are rugged enough to withstand most pets walking through them and using them for their personal hygiene. A low fence, such as the 12-inch-high white or green wire bed-edging fences can keep a small dog out of the prized flower bed, but may not do the trick for a headstrong or large dog. The underground electric "invisible fence" that is most often used to keep Fido on your property can also be used to keep him out of certain areas within the property.

Nothing is quite so magical as a dewy spiderweb catching the rays of the early morning light. Unless the web is absolutely in your way, do not disturb it. Spiders will catch many pest insects in their silken webs. Some spiders weave their webs daily, often eating the old one in the morning and spinning a new one by evening. Others leave their webs for a long time. Look closely and you may see several of their prey, wrapped in silk, hanging from the web, waiting to be the next meal.

It is interesting that many people feed the birds during the winter and then stop putting out seed as the weather warms in spring. Once you start giving birds seed, continue to do it year-round. Some birds switch to eating insects in spring—and will help control unwanted caterpillars and other creatures. Other birds prefer only seed; for them, it is a very lean period between the time people stop putting out seed and when garden plants begin to bear edible seeds. Baby birds, even those of seed eaters, cannot digest seed. Parent birds pick the area over looking for small insects, worms, and caterpillars for their hungry young. By providing seed for the adults, you encourage them to stay in your garden to forage for food for their chicks. Put up some birdhouses around the perimeter of your gardens in late winter, and you will have the pleasure of watching the birds raise one or more families during the growing season.

A compost pile is a must for every garden. Almost miraculously, it turns kitchen scraps (vegetable matter only), weeds, and garden waste into black gold, which you can spread throughout the garden to enrich the soil and fertilize the plants. Some gardeners go to great measures to board up, cover, and in a variety of ingenious ways, try to make the compost inaccessible to animals (mice, rats, and racoons are the main concerns). In making the pile impenetrable, you deprive it of air and water (rain or snow). The only compost piles I've ever known to really smell are those that have no air or insufficient moisture. Such piles also take much longer to rot. While the critters will get at some of the material in the compost pile, I would rather they ate that than the riches in my garden. Site your compost pile a good distance from the garden and house, and you shouldn't be bothered by any nocturnal feeders.

Previous page: *Sebastian loves catmint and other herbs*

April is like falling in love. It makes the old feel young and the young feel immortal. But a day of working the soil, transplanting, and mowing will restore your equilibrium ... at least until a night's sleep and another glorious, glistening day make you feel like dancing on the lawn, strewing rose petals, and shouting "Good morning!" to that curmudgeon of a neighbor.

Regions A, B, C, D, E April is a prime month for lectures on various gardening subjects, sponsored by botanical gardens, flower shows, home shows, public television stations, and major garden centers. They are often staged as a symposia, featuring local experts as well as nationally known authorities. Watch the calendar of events in your local newspaper. Lectures are a great place to pick up new ideas that start your creative juices flowing.

Regions A, B Start seeds of tender vegetables indoors for transplanting after danger of frost is past. Don't buy started seedlings until it is safe to plant them. Often cold, wet weather will hang around for many days, and seedlings can deteriorate while awaiting warm, dry weather.

Regions B, C Wet areas in your yard? You don't have to drain them. Adorn them with native American streamside plants such as ironweed, obedient plant, and cardinal flower.

Region E Don't let up on your control program for insects and plant diseases. Botanical and biological controls are available for most insects but not for plant diseases. Your best bet is to start with resistant varieties.

Dew highlights the spider's web

HINTS, CLUES, AND ADVICE

⌣ Have a good book to identify garden pests. Do not assume the cause of the damage without seeing the perpetrator in the act. Once identified, decide if the damage is sufficient to warrant treatment. Always try the least-toxic treatment first. Often handpicking or dousing with a strong spray of water works.

Regions A, B, C Days are growing much longer and brighter. Repot houseplants but wait two weeks before feeding them. Remember to keep a pitcher of water at room temperature for watering plants; water comes out of the faucet so cold that it can shock plants.

Regions B, C, D, E Mow often; let the clippings decompose in place. If you bag clippings, dump them in your compost pile after they have dried a day and have been turned. Wet succulent clippings can ferment and cause bad odors.

Regions B, C, D Want to harvest vegetables all summer? Plant lima beans, southern peas, sweet potatoes, melons, okra, and successive plantings of sweet corn and green beans. All of these are sensitive to cold soil, cold wind, and frost; wait until frost danger is past before planting. Melons are the most sensitive.

Region E Install high-quality edging around beds. Rolled-edge, heavy-duty plastic is reasonably durable, but heavy-gauge steel is the best. "Bender board" for edging is sold in the West.

Bee on Trachelium

HINTS, CLUES, AND ADVICE

⌁ Place a 6- or 8-inch clay pot upside down, propped open on one side with a rock or stone, in a cool corner of the garden. This makes a wonderful home for a toad. For the most part, it will be unseen, but a toad eats mosquitos and other insect pests. An added bonus is hearing it at night calling to other toads.

⌁ In winter, place chicken wire or bird netting on the soil in the area you do not want your pet to go. Their sensitive paws are uncomfortable walking on the fine wire or net, and by winter's end, they will be trained to avoid the area, and you can remove the wire for spring planting.

Region A Order seeds to grow long-stemmed garden flowers for use in fresh or dried flower arrangements. Only a few mail-order houses offer seeds of old-fashioned flowers for cutting; modern plant breeding seems to focus on developing short, large-flowered variations on the original.

Region A, B, C, D Do you live in an older home where "foundation plantings" from decades ago have grown to obscure windows and block out light? While it is possible to open up conifers and broad-leaved evergreens by severe pruning, you will have to continue it as long as the oversized plants live. Bite the bullet: cut down the monster shrubs, and dig out the roots. Amend the soil and start over with choice dwarf shrubs set out the proper distance from the house. How they will improve the appearance and apparent age of your house!

Region D If you live in the dry Southwest, don't aspire to an English landscape or Eastern cottage garden. Neither is appropriate. Instead, shop at nurseries that offer a good selection of native Southwestern wildflowers, shrubs, and trees that can take dry weather, scorching winds, and rapid changes in winter temperatures. Keep your lawn to the minimum by emphasizing groups of shrubs underplanted with wildflowers.

Region E To control slugs and snails without endangering children and pets, put the metalhyde bait in tin cans mashed nearly flat. Moisten the bait slightly to activate it. Or put stale beer in a shallow pan or tunfish can. Diatomaceous earth scattered around vulnerable plants is effective but needs to be reapplied after rains.

Destructive snail

HINTS, CLUES, AND ADVICE

🌙 Ducks may be attractive in a pond, but they are a messy addition to a swimming pool. To deter them, place several rubber or inflatable snakes (available at garden centers) around the perimeter of the pool. Change their positions every day so the ducks think they are alive. This has even worked to foil a great blue heron that started to feast on the koi I had just put into a small pond.

Regions A, B, C, D, E　Bats provide cheap insect control. If you have a few trees on your place, hang a bat house about 15 feet up. Paint a broad stripe of sticky Tanglefoot, or wrap duct tape (sticky side out) about 10 feet off the ground, to discourage cats from disturbing the day-sleeping bats.

Regions A, B, C, D　When planting a small yard consider tiny edging hostas for shade and dwarf daylilies for sunny spots. Think of your small yard as the land of the Munchkins (à la the Wizard of Oz), where all the elements are in miniature.

Regions B, C, D　Review your herb garden. Grow a good selection of savory herbs for soups, stews, and meat dishes and lighter-flavored herbs for salads, fruit dishes, drinks, and desserts. Remember the gray or silver-leaved herbs for lighting up landscapes.

Region E　Is your compost heap just sitting there, gaining size but not decomposing? It probably needs you to turn it, to add an activator such as chicken or sheep manure, and to wet each layer thoroughly as you rebuild it. If the pile seems quite loose, it may be drying out too fast. Stand atop it (careful, now!) and walk around (oops! compost heaps don't have handles) to reduce the air within it. Lay a sheet of plastic loosely over it to concentrate heat and reduce water loss.

TIP OF THE MONTH:
Hardly ever will you find a completely new idea in gardening or landscaping; home horticulture is slowly evolving, with most ideas, plants, and products seeming to piggyback on earlier developments. One of the best sources of state-of-the-art information is The Avant Gardener, a newsletter that has been produced for nearly 30 years. Contact the publisher at P.O. Box 489, New York City, NY 10028.

*Red Admiral butterfly on giant
allium*

HINTS, CLUES, AND ADVICE

⌒ Cats like catmint and catnip—mine also fancies a
good roll in the oregano. I like these plants in the garden, but don't appreciate a 15-pound cat rolling around
them, squashing other foliage in the process. Now I
plant them in a whiskey barrel, where Sebastian can feel
free to enjoy their scents without damaging other garden
treasures.

⌒ A nearby beehive increases your yield of many vegetables and fruit. In return for letting them keep the hive
on your property, beekeepers will often supply you with
as much honey as you can use.

MAY

result of mixing two primary colors. For example, green is a mixture of the two primary colors yellow and blue.

Complementary colors are directly opposite each other on the color wheel—blue and orange, yellow and violet, red and green. Harmonizing colors are adjacent to one another on the wheel, sharing a pigment—such as yellow, orange, and red (either two primary colors and the resulting secondary color, or two secondary colors and the common primary color).

It also helps to understand the dimensions that make one color unique from another. Hue distinguishes one named color from another—i.e., green from blue or blue from violet. Hue is defined as the pure color, without any white, black, or gray. Value is the degree of luminosity of a color—the lightness and darkness of a color. Value is divided into tints (the pure color mixed with varying amounts of white) and shades (the pure color mixed with varying amounts of black). The third dimension of color is intensity or saturation—a measure of the relative color—dull or bright, achieved by mixing the pure color with varying amounts of gray.

Much of color appreciation is subjective, and tastes vary widely. Perhaps you want a bright, vibrant garden. Select plants from the warm end of the spectrum (red, orange, yellow). You can also punctuate an orange flower with a planting of blue foliage next to it; blue and orange are complementary colors, so set each other off brilliantly. The bright violet of fall asters is made even more impressive when set next to goldenrod. Consider the values and intensity of the leaves of the plants—in most cases you'll be seeing the leaves much longer than the flowers.

Monochromatic gardens have been fashionable since Vita Sackville West did her now-famous white garden at Sissinghurst. I have heard of someone creating a black garden—too somber for my taste. A sunny yellow garden, mixing different values of yellows is fun to imagine in the cold of winter. Echo the color of the flowers in the foliage of nearby plants—black-eyed Susans with the variegated foliage of 'Gold Dust' aucuba.

You can literally work from both ends of the color spectrum, playing with tints and shades, intensities, and hues. Try planting as one gardener does—literally a color wheel in the corner of the garden, and then get ideas for other garden beds based on the plants in the wheel. In that type of planting the wheel is complex, with the shades and tints of each hue included in its segment, from palest tint to deepest shade, with pure hue in the center of each pie-shaped wedge.

Color and Texture for Contrast

What makes any garden interesting are the contrasts within it. These contrasts come from the hardscape, within the landscape, and how the two interact. To understand the contrasts, try taking a black-and-white picture (literally or in your mind's eye) of your garden. Strip away the colors, and you are looking at black, white, and varying intensities of gray. Look at the various plants without the distraction of the colors, and it is their form and texture, juxtaposed with one another and the hardscape that makes them appealing. A yucca, for instance, has a wonderful strong form, with its bold, sword-like leaves. It is best seen in profile, placed near a light-colored wall, sihouetted against the sky, or in a low, massed ground cover. Don't conceal it among other perennials of the same size.

Use similar shapes of different sizes for interest. The large heart-shaped leaves of a hosta are a good foil for the small heart-shaped, dainty leaves and flowers of spring violets. The hostas are just emerging from the ground at that time, so they won't overpower the violets.

In a desert garden, any cactus makes a statement by itself. It can be more fun to plant a low-growing, rounded spiny cactus in front of a tall, smoother cactus like a prickly pear. The juxtaposition of plants allows you to appreciate the texture of each more than if they were planted alone.

Now it's time to bring the other element back into the garden. You can have fun with a box of crayons and several copies of the same black-and-white garden scene or group of flowers. You can understand colors best by working with them—start with crayons before you get into actual plantings. Use a box of 64 colors to achieve the effects described here.

Color theory is based on a color wheel—a circle, equally divided into six pie-shaped pieces. Clockwise from the top, the colors are yellow, green, blue, violet, red, and orange. Yellow, blue, and red are primary colors. Green, violet, and orange are secondary colors—the

Previous page: *Contrasts and harmony*—Crocosmia, Rudbeckia, Perilla, Heliopsis, Coreopsis, and Dianthus.

There is no busier month for gardeners than May, but keep a positive attitude so that chores, no matter how tedious, are regarded as a learning experience or as healthful exercise. Northern soils are finally dry and warm enough to work for planting after frost danger, and farther south, weed seeds are sprouting everywhere. But the weather is so beautiful that, in your garden, the gain seems to come without pain.

Regions A, B, C, D, E Nothing improves plant growth on heavy clay soils like raised beds. Prepare them by digging the soil, spreading a 2-inch layer of sharp sand or granite meal and 2 inches of pulverized pine bark or peat moss, and mixing it thoroughly with the soil.

Regions A, B, C, Hang sticky artificial apples in fruit trees to trap insects whose eggs hatch into burrowing grubs.

Regions A, B, C, D Feed lawns with one of the new extended-release fertilizers to avoid overstimulating growth.

Region E Azaleas love acidic soil and humid air, thus are difficult to grow in the alkaline soils of the arid West. If and when you buy new azaleas, examine your soil. If it is heavy clay, work it up, set the root balls of the new azaleas atop it, then fill around them with sandy soil modified with organic matter. Potting soil topped with mulch will also work well. Azaleas have a shallow, dense root system and can't stand being planted in a poorly drained "bathtub" dug in heavy clay soil.

Asters and goldenrod

HINTS, CLUES, AND ADVICE

~ Keeping the overall picture of your ideal garden in mind, make a list of the plants you want to include. Scrutinize the list, checking to see if the flower colors work well together. Make sure you have a broad enough range of plant material to keep the garden interesting year-round.

~ Silver foliage plants are excellent for cooling down hot flower colors. In the dog days of August, you will appreciate the refreshing effect of the silver leaves. Use silver foliage or white flowers to separate colors that would otherwise clash.

Region A Buy tender bedding plants and perennials early to get a good choice, but don't risk planting them until after frost danger is past.

Regions A, B, C, D, E How good a landlord are you to the toads in your garden? Have you set toad houses here and there? You can buy special terra cotta or wood toad shelters, or you can make your own of "hypertufa," a blend of Portland Cement, peat moss, perlite, co-polymer fibers, liquid acrylic bonding agent, and water. Make a barely moist mixture like bread dough and press it to a depth of $1\frac{1}{2}$ inches inside a 12-inch-diameter plastic bowl. After 24 hours, tip it out, carve out a low door, and let it cure in the shade for a few weeks. Rain will leach away the harsh alkalinity. Lightweight hypertufa will not radiate too much heat for toad comfort and will hold up against freezing and thawing.

Regions A, B, C Turn the leaves accumulated last fall and mix grass clippings with them to kick off the hot composting needed to kill weed and grass seeds. Keep the heat stoked with turning and watering. Compost heaps need a certain "critical mass" to maintain internal heat; they should be at least 3 feet high and 4 feet across.

Regions D, E Orchid growing is really catching on in mild-winter climates, where the tropicals are grown in heated shelters and where the cool-loving terrestrials can be grown with minimum protection. Lifetime collections of high-quality orchids can represent significant sums of money and are virtually irreplaceable; before next winter, be sure to have a backup heating system ready in the event of power failure or extreme cold. Growing orchids without one is like playing Russian roulette.

Barrel cactus, Echinocactus grusonii

HINTS, CLUES, AND ADVICE

✂ Include plants for year-round interest in the garden. Look to evergreens—needled or broad-leafed—for color and texture. The form of a small deciduous plant, like a Japanese maple or Harry Lauder's walking stick, gives interest, especially without its leaves. These permanent plants also provide a place for beneficial insects (praying mantis in particular) to lay eggs or overwinter.

Regions A, B, C, D Don't discard overripe bananas. Split them and lay them in the garden for butterflies to feed on their fermenting juices.

Regions A, B, C, D Level soil can be prepared for new vegetable beds by "solarizing." Work up the soil, and then cover it with plastic, burying the edges in a shallow ditch. In about 8 weeks, remove the plastic. Solar heat will kill most weed and grass seeds to a depth of 6 inches.

Regions A, B, C As your perennials and shrubs emerge, label all whose name and source you can remember. Include the year planted, if you can recall it. Keep a supply of metal labels handy to mark your new acquisitions. But make a map of each perennial or shrub bed as well, to identify plants when labels have been scattered by deer or pets, raked away during winter cleanup, or lost beneath mulch.

Region D "Florida flowers" are moving north into the middle and upper South. When visiting your local garden center, look for multicolored pentas (Egyptian star cluster flowers), golden melampodium, mandevilla, bougainvillea, chenille plant, and tropical hibiscus, to name a few. They are very resistant to heat and humidity.

Region E Feed your lawn again. High heat combined with heavy rainfall or irrigation makes frequent feeding necessary, especially on sandy, easily leached soils. The new generation of controlled-release lawn fertilizers will eliminate "feast or famine" plant nutrition cycles.

Giant allium and mint

HINTS, CLUES, AND ADVICE

~ When choosing a plant for its texture, consider the distance from which the garden or plant is generally viewed. For example, the finely textured form of some ferns cannot be appreciated from far away. A boldly architectural plant like a yucca is easily admired from both near and far.

Regions A, B, C, D This is your dermatologist speaking: "Buy and wear a broad-brimmed hat and apply a sunblock before venturing into your garden."

Region D When installing a wildflower meadow, clean up the soil by solarizing, repeated tillage, or three applications made a month apart of a nonselective herbicide. In the fall, buy plants and set them out 2 or 3 feet apart. Broadcast wildflower seeds between the plants.

Region E Check your citrus trees and tropical fruits for signs of insect damage. Scale insects are most vulnerable to sprays when they have come out of winter dormancy and are on the move.

TIP OF THE MONTH:

Prune spring-flowering shrubs after they have bloomed. If you wait until winter to prune them, you will cut off many of the bloom buds formed during the summer. Late fall or winter pruning is okay for most summer- blooming shrubs because they bloom on woody growth formed during late spring and summer. Timely pruning maximizes flower production. Pruning is more than shaping. It includes thinning congested shrubs and thickety clumps by removing weak, contorted, or contrary stems at the base. High-quality, articulated, double-action loppers (long-handled shears) work well for thinning, but you will probably need a slender, curved pruning saw as well. One try at wrestling with a congested shrub with a bucksaw and hand shears will send you straightaway to your local garden center to upgrade your tools.

Hosta with violets

HINTS, CLUES, AND ADVICE

⌒ If you are charmed into impulsively buying a great plant at a nursery or from a catalogue, when you get it home, set it (do not plant yet) in the garden where you think you want it. If it's not in bloom, make some colored circles the same colors the flowers will be and lay them on the leaves. Take the plant to several other possible locations to see how it compares. This will give you a chance to see what characteristics of the plant you want to show off and the best spot for doing that. This method saves a lot of needless work and replanting— you'll be surprised how often you find the original location isn't the best.

JUNE

Vertical Gardens—Growing Up

Whether you are a city, suburban, or country gardener, whether you have a condominium with a only a small terrace, a house with an average backyard, or a sprawling estate, you will create a more interesting space by going vertical. Vertical gardening is practical. By maximizing space, the plants do not take up valuable ground—potential growing space—for anything but their roots and stems. Plants grown vertically are generally healthier than those allowed to sprawl on the ground, benefiting from increased air circulation and a greater number of leaves exposed to the sunlight.

Vines are the most common plants to grow vertically. Although some like *Euonymus* and ivies make good ground covers, when they are given support they reach for the sky and make superlative wall covers. Vines are versatile—softening stark architectural lines, providing a screen for shade and/or privacy, and extending limited garden space. Don't overlook the fact that they move the focal point up adding to the diversity of the garden.

Vines can be divided into two basic types—clinging and non-clinging. The advantage to clinging vines is that they can hold on to most any surface without your help. For example, Boston ivy's short tendrils have suction cup-like disks at the ends, allowing it to easily attach to almost any surface without damage. Small, root-like hold-fasts along the stems of climbing hydrangea, English ivy, creeping fig, wintercreeper, and trumpet vine make for strong vertical growth. They do best on slightly rough surfaces like brick, wood, or stone and even like to climb tree trunks. Climbers can transform an unsightly chain-link fence into a thing of beauty for all seasons with a combination of evergreen vines like ivy or wintercreeper and some summer flowering trumpet vine.

The other group of vines—non-clinging vines—have unique methods of pulling themselves off the ground, as long as you provide vertical support. Twining vines weave themselves around the support. Star jasmine, a delightfully fragrant, delicate vine will twine around and through a lattice. Wisteria, a vigorous vine that can grow 40 to 50 feet, requires a very sturdy support, like a broad arbor or pergola. A word of caution—although it may be tempting to let a wisteria wind its way up a tree, in time it will strangle and kill the tree. Other non-clinging vines, like peas and grapes, hang on by means of tendrils that tightly coil around narrow supports. Wooden trellises, wires, netting, and strings are best. Don't be deceived by their dainty look—the tendrils are surprisingly strong. At the end of the growing season, I use pruners to cut down the vigorous annual moonflower vine rather than risk tearing apart a trellis.

Some long-stemmed plants, like climbing roses, are not true vines. They must have assistance to propel themselves upward. With the help of a support and some ties to loosely attach the stems or canes, they make a beautiful vertical accent.

The last group of plants for a vertical garden are espaliers, trees or shrubs that have an upright habit by themselves, and, with training, can be flattened into growing against a wall or trellis. Even in limited space, you can grow espaliered fruit trees—dwarf or standard size. A recent apple introduction, 'Colonnade,' needs no training—and will grow in any sunny 2' by 2', producing a single trunk up to 8' tall with no long side branches and very tasty apples. Magnolias, forsythia, and pyracantha are handsome ornamentals that are fun to train as espalier. Some nurseries specialize in espalier trees, doing all the training, so all you have to do is put the plant in the ground, water it, and keep it pruned.

In a small sunny space, you can grow a bountiful harvest of fruits and vegetables. Besides espalier fruit trees, train cucumbers, squash, beans, and peas on wires, trellises, poles, or even netting strung between two poles or stakes. Stake tomatoes to grow upward instead of sprawling.

The supporting players in the vertical garden add to its beauty and splendor. A gazebo, resplendent with morning glory and fragrant moonflowers climbing up its posts, is a magic place from which to enjoy the rest of the garden. A pergola provides shade while supporting even strong climbers like wisteria, grape, or hydrangea. Add a romantic touch with a rose arbor. Even a simple picket fence is softened and transformed with fragrant sweet peas twining among the pickets.

In Pennsylvania I saw what looked like and oversized, 20-foot, metal birdcage. It was an old corncrib, put to a new use, with hardy kiwi climbing all up and over it. What a delight to walk inside and pick the ripe, large grape sized fruits.

Previous page: *Climbing roses arch above a garden gateway*

In a well-planned garden, everything comes together in June. Colors from annuals replace the azaleas in Southern gardens, perennials begin their summer show, and a steady stream of fresh vegetables flows into your kitchen. The fragrance of herbs wafts across the garden on warm breezes. Butterflies hatch or return from their migrations, and hummingbirds defend their feeding grounds against all comers. For gardeners, it's a positive time, with few disappointments or difficulties.

Regions A, B, C, D, E Try the new biological insecticides based on neem tree oil for controlling soft-bodied insects such as whiteflies and aphids.

Regions A, B, C, D, E Sow buckwheat seeds in idle parts of your garden to snuff out weeds while producing green matter to be worked into the soil to enrich it.

Regions A, B, C, D, E Enchant children with an arbor hideaway covered with lush, colorful scarlet runner bean vines. Farther south, try an arbor of coral vine.

Regions A, B, C, D Dissatisfied with the way your garden looks? The greatest improvement at the least cost can come with sizable containers of flowers, vegetables, or herbs set at various heights at critical points in your landscape.

Region E Don't surrender to the running bamboos and let them take over your garden. Snap off the growing points of the culms, or mow them off to stop bamboo's spread.

Alyssum and phlox atop a wall

HINTS, CLUES, AND ADVICE

∿ Check out your house before planting a climbing vine next to it. Especially in houses with old or soft masonry, the rootlets of some climbers can work their way in and weaken the mortar betweem the bricks or stones. How many of the venerable ivy-covered brick institutions of New England would crumble if the ivy were pulled off?

Regions A, B, C, D, E Weed problems are directly proportional to the amount of bare ground in gardens. Mulch between flower plants with leaves or bark mulch and between vegetable rows with grass clipping laid on sheets of newspaper.

Region A Expect occasional cold nights. Keep floating row covers handy to ward off frost.

Regions A, B, C Don't try to grow lawn grass beneath surface-rooted trees. Instead, mow the lawn close, and spread 2 to 3 inches of mulch over newspapers or cardboard. Plant ground cover through the mulch.

Region C Azaleas are hard to resist, blooming in brilliant blocks of color at garden centers. But their very popularity creates overplanting, their major disadvantage. Overplanting is most obvious, even irritating, in vivid purple, pink, and cerise. In many gardens, the summer landscape is all green: the azaleas have bloomed and have sent out new green foliage, the broad-leaved evergreen shrubs bloom but you'd never know it, and the major kinds of ground covers are solid green. How boring! How inconsiderate of the butterflies and hummingbirds that need food sources! So, be conservative in the number of azaleas you buy, and discriminating in the colors you choose.

Region D You may be charmed by the rhododendrons now in bloom in garden centers, and they are extravagantly beautiful. They grow best in beds of sandy, well-drained, fairly acidic soil. In dry climates, rhododendrons benefit from frequent light irrigations from overhead sprinklers.

Region E Too much sun in gardens can be a problem in the deep South and West. Erect a lath or shadecloth structure to give you a pleasant place to rest and to display plants that prefer moderate shade. Or plant a drought-resistant native tree.

Passionflower vine

HINTS, CLUES, AND ADVICE

↘ Some vines can grow at prodigious rates, quickly covering up windows or doorways. Try to lead the vine away from areas you want kept clear. To keep third-story windows free of ivy, it may be easier to prune from the inside, working out, rather than getting on a very tall ladder.

Regions A, B, C, D, E Consider joining the Perennial Plant Association. Its members try up-and-coming cultivars and rate them for performance. Each year the association announces the "Perennial Plant of the Year." Some of the previous winners include *Astilbe* 'Sprite', *Coreopsis* 'Moonbeam', and *Heuchera* or coral bells 'Palace Purple'. You'll find the organization's address and many others in Barbara Barton's *Gardening by Mail*, perhaps the most complete national source book for plants, seeds, garden products, and gardening organizations.

Regions A, B, C, D, E June is a good time to look at your garden to see if it could be improved by adding structures: arbors, fences, dry streams, water features, or benches.

Regions A, B, C Warm soil means it's time to plant basil seeds. Dig a shallow furrow, sprinkle the seeds thinly, and step on them to press them into the soil. They will sprout in 7 to 10 days and grow quickly into sturdy plants.

Region D Dry weather may be stunting your flowers, drying up your food garden, and hurting fruit and nut trees. Install drip irrigation. It reduces water use by as much as 30 percent while improving the condition of flowers, vegetables, shrubs, and trees and while reducing the chance of foliage diseases brought on by watering with sprinklers.

Region E Don't overlook fragrance in your garden. Ginger lilies smell sweet, yet are not overpowering.

Climbing roses

HINTS, CLUES, AND ADVICE

∽ Create a fun place for kids in the garden. Build a tepee from six bamboo stakes (6 to 8 feet tall) and plant scarlet runner beans and 'Jack-Be-Little' pumpkins at the base of the stakes. Kids love to sit in the tepee and watch you at work in the garden. They will marvel at how fast the beans and pumpkins grow up the stakes, creating a neat hidey-hole for them that has red edible flowers, delicious beans and tiny Jack-o'-lanterns all over the outside.

Regions A, B, C   Now's the time to visit a botanical or estate garden in your region to see the newest and best perennials in full bloom. Actually, you'll need to make a second visit in about two months to catch the late-blooming species.

Regions A, B, C, D, E   If you have a water garden, stand back and look at it. If it consists mostly of a liner with a single line of coping stones to hide the top, it can't be very attractive, even if it holds a wonderful assortment of plants and/or fish. Buy large containers in short, medium, and tall shapes, and group them just off the edge of the coping where they look the best. Fill them with good-grade nursery mix and plant with streamside flowers such as cardinal flower, obedient plant, turtlehead, ironweed, jewelweed, or other native plants adapted to your climate. Butterflies and hummingbirds will flock to them, adding a whole new dimension of action to your water feature.

TIP OF THE MONTH:

Before you invest in a lot of power equipment, ask yourself if your garden really needs it and if you have a place to park it while not in use. Rental rates on large power equipment are high, but rental is a good option compared with the expense and work of maintaining seldom used equipment. Part of enjoying a garden comes from the honest work required to maintain a lively and graceful landscape and a productive patch of food plants. In gardening and landscaping, the process—the means to an end—should bring you satisfaction, not just the results.

Climbing snapdragon

HINTS, CLUES, AND ADVICE

⌒ When growing large fruiting vines like melon or squash vertically, provide support for the fruit so its weight does not pop it off the vine before it ripens. Try old stockings or pantyhose tied on the trellis. Be sure the trellis itself is well anchored so the maturing fruit-laden vine doesn't pull it down.

J ULY

Edible Flowers for Beauty and Flavor

Have you ever eaten a flower? The answer is probably yes; you just may be unaware of how many flowers are part of common foods and beverages. Artichokes are immature flowers. If you've grown broccoli, you've seen the green flower buds elongate and open into yellow flowers (which are delicious). Dried daylily buds (golden needles) are standard ingredients in Chinese hot and sour soup. Many herbal teas are made with flowers. Read the ingredients listed on the side of the boxes in your kitchen and you may see rose petals, hibiscus, mint, chamomile, and other familiar flowers. As a child, do you remember sucking the nectar from honeysuckle blossoms? Try it again—it tastes just as sweet.

The reintroduction of flowers into cuisine began on the West Coast in the 1970s. I say reintroduction, because edible flowers have a long history. The Chinese have been using daylilies and chrysanthemums for several millennia. Ancient Romans introduced many herbs into their kitchens and added cultivated flowers, including mallows, roses, and violets to their culinary repertoire. Most European and Asian cuisines use flowers with regularity. Squash blossoms are common in Italian cooking. Many Indian and Middle Eastern dishes make use of orange, rose, and jasmine flowers. Unfortunately, in America, by the 1920s, we had all but forgotten about using flowers to enhance food.

Today, despite the resurgence of interest in edible flowers, people are unaware of their great variety. Pansies and nasturtiums commonly show up on salads in restaurants, yet there are at least 70 other flowers (and hundreds of species and hybrids of those 70) that are a wonderful addition to any cuisine. You probably have some growing in your garden right now—lilacs, roses, hibiscus, chrysanthemums, calendulas, Johnny jump-ups, and flowers from many herbs.

Edible flowers are in culinary class of their own, technically neither spices nor herbs (although some are herb flowers). The range of flavors is broad—bland, spicy, sweet, piquant, peppery, perfumed, oniony, bitter, herbal, minty, floral, citrusy, and anise. Most can be eaten raw.

In addition to the flavors they impart to a dish, edible flowers add color, especially as a garnish on a dish flavored with flowers. Every hue of the rainbow is represented. I know of no easier way to convert family food into company fare than by adding flowers. For impressive hors d'oeuvres, I serve nasturtiums stuffed with flowered cheese (whipped cream cheese flavored and colored with minced flower petals) and crudités surrounding a hibiscus flower filled with a favorite dip. A good way to introduce most flowers into your food is to chop them up and watch how they liven up a salad, visually and taste-wise.

To many people, and food professionals in particular, flowers are merely a garnish. However, if a flower is on a dish with food, it should be safe to eat. *If a flower is not on the list in the appendix, don't eat it.* Like wild mushrooms, some flowers are truly culinary delights, some have little flavor, others taste bad, and a few are poisonous.

Some natural chemicals responsible for scent and flavor are more concentrated in the blossom. Other substances become more concentrated in the flower, too, especially fertilizers, pesticides, and even herbicides applied to the surrounding soil. For that reason, *flowers should only be eaten from organic gardens.* Never get them as cut flowers from a florist; leave those in a vase, not on a plate.

Pick flowers in the cool of the day, preferably in early morning. Like fruit, unripe and overripe flowers do not have the superb flavor of those at their peak. Ignore those not fully open, past their prime, or starting to wilt. Immediately after picking, put long-stemmed flowers into water in a cool place. Pick short-stemmed blossoms, such as borage and orange blossoms, no more than three or four hours before using and put them between layers of damp paper toweling or in a plastic bag in the refrigerator. Immediately before using, gently wash the flowers, checking carefully for bugs and dirt.

Only your imagination and flavor preferences limit the possibilities for using edible flowers in cuisine. They are truly flowers for beauty and taste, adding beauty to both garden and food, while reflecting the good taste of the gardener who plants them and the cook who uses them in the kitchen.

Previous page: *An edible flower garden*

Bathed in the strongest sunlight of the year, golden July is a time when gardeners would like just to stand back and watch things grow. This month, however, demands much care in return for its beauty. Lounge in your hammock or snooze on the porch during the midday heat, but venture out in the cool hours of early morning and evening for weeding, watering, insect control, and training errant vines.

Regions A, B, C, D, E   July is a good month to visit a nearby botanical or estate garden to see the latest cultivars of hostas or daylilies at their best. Write to the American Association of Botanical Gardens and Arboreta, 786 Church Road, Wayne, PA 19087, for a list of gardens and arboreta in your area.

Region A   Feed your lawn again. If it responds poorly, it may need thatching and coring. Thatching removes accumulated dead grass; coring pulls out cigar-like plugs of soil to improve aeration. You can rent machines or hire someone to do the work.

Region A   If you applied floating row covers early on to protect against frost and insect depredations, consider removing them now to prevent the temperature underneath from rising too high.

Regions B, C   For tasty hors d'oeuvres, soak ready-to-open daylily buds in water (to float away insects in hiding). Stuff the buds with a mixture of cream cheese and chopped nuts

Region E   On the West Coast, visit the advanced independent nurseries that carry the newest in flowers developed in foreign countries or by domestic plant breeders: cat's claw *Orthosiphon,* scaveola, supertunias, and the incredible blue *Oxypetalum caeruleum,* to name just a few.

Violets

H I N T S ,   C L U E S ,   A N D   A D V I C E

⌁ If there is any question as to the identity of a flower, err on the side of caution and do not eat it. Just because the flower is on your plate at a fancy restaurant, do not assume that the chef or server knows that the flower is edible. I have been served a few toxic flowers in restaurants. Sometimes a chef may think that if any flower is grown organically it can be eaten—that is not true.

Regions A, B, C, D, E Most states have statewide wild-flower or native plant societies. One of the best-kept secrets in horticulture is that many such societies operate "seed exchanges." You don't have to join these organizations to order seeds of a great range of North American wildflowers and seeds of a few native trees and shrubs. Their members collect seeds from plentiful native stands or from blocks of individual species they grow for seed production. Request a list of wildflower or native seed sources from the National Wildflower Research Center, headquartered at 4801 Lacrosse Avenue, Austin, TX 78739-1702. They will send you an order form that lists all the information available.

Regions A, B, C At midmonth, direct-seed fall greens and root crops in your vegetable garden; also sow second crops of dill, chervil, cilantro, cress, and arugula.

Regions A, B, C Hang baskets of shade-tolerant flowers from the lower branches of trees to brighten dark and cheerless areas.

Regions B, C, D Kill those pesky flea beetles with the botanical insecticide rotenone. They can riddle the leaves of certain plants, especially eggplants and potatoes, with pinhead-sized holes.

Regions D, E Remove spent or leggy annual flowers and replace them with heat-resistant pentas, melampodium, rose moss, or tropical salvias such as *Salvia coccinea*.

Nasturtium 'Alaska' and Dianthus

HINTS, CLUES, AND ADVICE

⌒ Only the petals of most flowers are edible. Some, however, including Johnny jump-up, violet, runner bean, honeysuckle, and clover can be eaten in their entirety. When using just the petals, separate them from the rest of the flower just before using to keep wilting to a minimum. Some flower petals, such as roses, yucca, dianthus, marigolds, and mums, have a bitter portion near where the petal was attached, which should be removed before eating. Always remove pistils and stamens from flowers.

Regions A, B, C, D, E There's still time to get a lot of enjoyment from a strawberry jar planted with herbs. The trouble with most preplanted herb jars is that they are too small; they dry out quickly and stunt the growth of plants. Start with a 3- to 5-gallon strawberry jar, and plant it with herbs that are small when mature. Standard sweet basil, for example, will rapidly overgrow any container that holds less than 10 gallons. Little 'Spicy Globe', on the other hand, will stay within bounds. Mix one of the controlled-release fertilizers with your potting soil; your plants will be fed for several months from a single application.

Regions A, B, C, D, E If you have a bug-zapper light, retire it. These lights kill very few mosquitoes while eliminating many insect predators and species essential to pollination.

Regions C, D Tomatoes often drop off drastically in production because of hot nights, which inhibit pollination. Set out new plants for a fall crop. If you have trouble with tomatoes dying because of nematodes, or eggplants expiring to complexes of soil diseases, grow them in containers filled with artificial soil and set up on bricks to keep organisms from entering the container through the drainage holes. Add pelleted dolomitic lime to the potting mix at the rate of $\frac{1}{4}$ pound lime per gallon of mix.

Region E Western and Southwestern gardeners often have trouble with the top 3 or 4 inches of container mixes drying out and refusing to reabsorb water. Rectify the situation by adding $\frac{1}{4}$ teaspoon of a mild detergent to a gallon of water and gradually sprinkling it over the dry mix. The "wetter water" will soak into the mix, and it will continue to take up water for two or three weeks, allowing roots to establish in the formerly dry zone.

Sage with violets

HINTS, CLUES, AND ADVICE

⌒ Get to know the edible flowers by botanic name. Common names, although sometimes descriptive, vary from one region to another. Calendula, a lovely flower that can be used as a saffron substitute, is also known as pot marigold. However, it is not a marigold. In fact, most marigolds, with the exception of the single French marigolds like 'Lemon Gem' and 'Tangerine Gem' (which have a citrusy tarragon flavor), are inedible.

Regions A, B, C, D, E When germinating seeds in hot dry soil, scatter them in a shallow furrow after filling it with water and letting it soak in. Cover with a board. Seeds will sprout quickly in the warm, moist environment.

Regions A, B, C Whiteflies on tomatoes and marigolds can reduce their vigor and transmit systemic diseases. Kill them with one of the new biological insecticides containing neem oil.

Region E Consider the palm-like cycads as bold foliage plants. They require minimal care and can get by with little supplementary watering.

TIP OF THE MONTH:

If you have a greenhouse or cold frame, move plants to a shaded area in the garden, disinfect all interior surfaces of your structure, and kill insect eggs with a light, emulsifiable oil, using a pump sprayer. Despite good ventilation, during the summer greenhouses usually run at least 10 degrees hotter than outside air. This is why gardeners in the South and warm West don't build greenhouses as lean-tos on their homes; they raise the cost of air conditioning. Southern and Western greenhouses can benefit from evaporative pad cooling, which draws air through a moistened pad of decay-resistant fiber or corrugated fiber board.

An edible flower bouquet

HINTS, CLUES, AND ADVICE

⤳ If you have hay fever, asthma, or allergies, do not eat flowers. Introduce flowers into your diet the way you would new foods to a baby—one at a time in small quantities. Like any other food, nothing says you have to like the flavor of all flowers.

⤳ Flowers may vary in taste when grown in different locations. Different varieties of the same flower are apt to taste different from one another. Never eat flowers picked from the side of the road as they are likely to be contaminated by car exhaust.

AUGUST

Evening Gardens—Gardens for Evening Enjoyment

With our busy schedules, there isn't enough time to spend working in the garden, much less relaxing and enjoying it. A simple solution is to create a garden that can be enjoyed when there is free time—from late afternoon through the night.

Darkness is a great advantage in a garden. It is hard to see weeds in the dark, so you feel no guilt about enjoying the garden. It takes about 20 minutes for your eyes to adjust to darkness, forcing you to slow down in the garden. In summer it is most enjoyable to sit outdoors with friends or family. Watch the garden and you'll find it is more entertaining than TV or video. You'll be surprised at the sights, sounds, and scents of the garden in the evening.

A garden planned for evening enjoyment is attractive during the day, but it really comes into its glory as the light fades. Bright flowers like black-eyed Susans and cardinal flowers glow in the warm light of the late afternoon. As the sun wanes, pale and cool-colored flowers like isotoma, cinneraria, and purple clematis take on a life of their own, seeming to fluoresce. As darkness descends, leaves with light-colored variegations stand out—variegated ivies are visible as ground covers while their deep green–leafed cousins become invisible. White and pale flowers appear to float in the air, their earthly attachments of green stems and leaves fading and blending into the surrounding darkness. White flowers like autumn clematis, sweet alyssum, and candytuft are visible even in the dimmest light—but during a full moon they really pop out of the landscape. Moonlight also accentuates plants with silver foliage like dusty miller, artemisia, lamb's ears, and even artichokes.

For pure sensory pleasure, I love to sit outside in the dark with the lights off and concentrate on the fragrances of my garden. The scents become headier as summer progresses and the white-flowered galtonias, tuberoses, and nicotiana (flowering tobacco) bloom.

Some flowers are fragrant only after the sun goes down, a scented lure for their nocturnal pollinators. What a thrill to see a luna moth, one of nature's magnificent creations, flitting around the garden phlox by moonlight.

The true stars of the evening garden are those flowers that open only at night. Mid to late summer brings out the moonflowers and angel's trumpets. After sunset, it is fascinating to watch moonflowers gradually unfurl until at last they burst open and fill the night air with their perfume. An individual moonflower or angel's trumpet blooms for a single night, closing up and withering when the light of day hits it (on a cloudy day the flowers stay open); however, the plant will keep producing flowers for many months. Four o'clocks may open later than their name implies, but their flowers are a great aromatic addition to the evening garden.

Make an effort to experience the garden as much as possible at night. The evening sounds of the garden are enchanting. Sitting by the pool I hear the rustling of the ornamental grasses in the breeze and the soughing of the tall pines.

In order to enjoy our gardens outdoors year-round, it is important to include more plants of architectural interest. Use trees and shrubs that have interesting shapes or bark to attract attention after the flowers are gone and at night. Ornamental grasses provide interest throughout the year.

Lighting plays a major role, whether it is just the light of the moon or outdoor lights, emphasizing plants and casting interesting shadows. Today, it is simple and affordable to create your own custom garden lighting using attractive, inexpensive, low-voltage, do-it-yourself garden lights. I have been pleased at the ease of installation and the varied effects I can create in the garden. Depending on your taste, garden and pathway lighting can be incredibly dramatic or subtle.

Night falls upon us all, so consider creating an evening garden. By combining plant material, lighting, and design, you can enjoy your garden as I do mine, at any time of day or night. Choose a spot for your evening garden that is easily visible—perhaps along the path from the garage to the house or a patch of garden you can see from your easy chair. See how the plants already in it look from late afternoon through twilight and into the dark of night, on moonless nights, and with a full moon. Include a range of plants so that the garden retains interest throughout the year.

An evening garden can be a private space for you to treasure alone or an area to share, relax and enjoy with friends and family.

Previous page: *Subtle garden lighting*

Incredibly, some gardeners would wish away the month of August. "Heat, humidity, bugs, and sunburn," they say, never rising early enough to enjoy the rustling and piping of songbirds just after sunrise, nor venturing out late to sort out the numerous species of toads and frogs by the calls emanating from ditches and ponds. They can't wait for vacation, then worry about their garden while they are away. To ease their fears, they need only to make out a schedule of things to do, and ask whoever will be caring for the garden to check off the chores as they are completed. The garden sitter won't be insulted if you explain that the checklist will make the job easier. The most likely chore to be overlooked is watering. You can make watering happen automatically, on time, and of the right duration, by installing drip irrigation controlled by a programmable timer. Long-lasting controlled-release fertilizers can nourish plants for months from a single application, eliminating another worry.

Regions A, B, C, D, E Scout your perennial flowers for seed pods. Sow the seeds in small containers of moist potting soil and set them in the fridge for a month. Then, put them in a warm spot and watch for sprouts. Some may not germinate until the following spring.

Region A Plant seeds of salad greens and pot herbs in a cold frame for fall harvest. Crack the lid to keep down interior temperatures during warm days.

Regions B, C Early in the month, direct-seed fall greens and pot herbs. To persuade seeds to emerge through dry soil, plant them in the bottom of 2-inch-deep furrows or cover them with burlap. Sprinkle with water twice daily until seeds germinate, then daily until seedlings have six leaves.

Regions B, C, D Want a change from chrysanthemums for fall color? Plant dwarf New England asters in blue, lavender, purple, pink, and white.

Region E You're right, it is hot! And you may be tempted to mow in the wee hours of morning to avoid the heat. Be a considerate neighbor; don't crank up the mower until dusk.

An inviting evening garden

HINTS, CLUES, AND ADVICE

∽ Start slowly—some of the best evening gardens evolve, rather than being overnight creations. Add several plants to your existing garden such as a dusty miller, variegated snow-on-the-mountain, moonflower vines, or nicotiana. As you get a feel for the garden, move out plants that do not pop out at night and add ones that grab your attention.

Regions A, B With a little extra thought you can construct a cold frame that will protect plants to 17 degrees F. Build it with foam-insulated boards, sheathed with foil, and make the top of two layers of clear plastic film separated by dead air space. Gaskets beneath the lid will help seal out cold winds. Starting this early should give you time to complete the project prior to winter.

Regions B, C Mid-August is the deadline for setting out plants of cabbage, broccoli, cauliflower, and Brussels sprouts to have them head up for harvest before a killing frost.

Region E Southern and Western gardeners can buy inexpensive terra cotta containers made in Mexico. These are fired at lower temperatures than the domestic product, so they tend to soak up water and self-destruct after a season or two. You can extend their life by coating the insides with liquid asphalt roofing compound.

Region E West Coast and desert lawns are often troubled by dry spots where grass struggles or dies. This may be due to soil compaction or to a "hardpan" from 6 to 12 inches below the surface. Before you dig up the area and modify the soil, try mixing a bit of horticultural surfactant in a watering can and sprinkling the dry spot with it. Apply the solution several times, an hour or two apart, to allow the "wetter water" to penetrate the dense layers. Be careful though: some detergents are phytotoxic. Your local garden center can recommend a surfactant that won't kill plants.

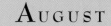

Moonflower

HINTS, CLUES, AND ADVICE

⟋ Moonflowers are my favorites for the garden. You can readily buy the seed. Soak the seeds overnight in tepid water and plant in the garden when the soil is warm (about the same time you would plant tomatoes), providing sturdy support for the vines to climb. Be patient: the plants do not take off until the weather gets hot. In the North they start to bloom at the beginning of August, continuing until frost.

Regions A, B Set out plants of ornamental kale and cabbage for fall color through Thanksgiving.

Region D August is a good time to select trees for your landscape, but it's about a month early for planting them. Trees are an important, long-term investment. Talk to the best nurseryman in your area about the smaller trees that deliver excellent form, along with colorful blooms or bright fall foliage. Look for berried trees if they are to be planted away from drives or walks; wild birds will benefit from your largesse. Avoid planting "cliché" trees that appear in landscapes all over town; one of these days a plague may strike them because of the overplanting.

Regions D, E In the South and warm West, fall is a better time for planting flowers and shrubs than spring. August is too early for soil preparation.

Region E My, does the yard waste pile up in warm-climate gardens, and many gardeners have it hauled off. How much kinder it would be to the environment to compost it quickly and efficiently in a hidden corner of your garden. There's nothing like a top dressing of compost to perk up debilitated plants. Practice the motto "Don't bag it!"

Soft color in an evening garden

HINTS, CLUES, AND ADVICE

∽ Use lighting judiciously. Walk around the garden and select one or two plants or small areas to highlight. Use uplighting to focus attention on these areas. Use more subtle techniques like sidelighting, downlighting, shadowing, and silhouetting to accentuate other parts of the garden.

Region A Begin harvesting herbs for freezing and drying—and stems of everlasting flowers for drying.

Regions B, C Deficiencies of calcium and magnesium
in garden and container soils may cause your tomatoes,
peppers, and eggplants to develop blossom-end rot.
Correct the situation by working a half cup of pelleted
or finely powdered lime into the soil around each plant.

Regions B, C Pull out tattered and woebegone annuals.
Replace them with quick-blooming sorts such as sweet
alyssum and cold-hardy pansies and calendulas.

Regions D, E It's time to direct-seed collards, turnips,
and mustard greens for fall and winter harvest. Ridge up
rows on heavy soil for better drainage and aeration.
Unless you garden on the West Coast, forget Brussels
sprouts, rutabagas, and most other root crops except
turnips; Southern winters are too harsh and variable for
good results. In coastal areas of the West Coast, special
varieties of cauliflower, broccoli, and Brussels sprouts have
been developed for harvest during winter and early spring
months, and plants can be set out now if watered well.

TIP OF THE MONTH:

The least-expensive way to add organic matter to
flower beds, vegetable gardens, and new areas that
are to be landscaped is to grow "green manure crops"
for turning under the following spring. Scatter seeds
of annual ryegrass among your vegetable rows or, in
Regions D and E, seeds of Austrian peas or crimson
clover. The plants will live through the winter to provide a substantial amount of green matter in their
tops and roots. When turned under, it will decompose to humus.

White tulips glow in an evening garden

HINTS, CLUES, AND ADVICE

∼ Create an instant winter evening garden by sticking some white birch branches (or other branches pruned from larger trees) in the ground. Keep small white holiday lights up year-round on one or two trees or shrubs. Turn them on occasionally to produce a festive mood.

SEPTEMBER

Shade—An Asset in the Landscape

When I started gardening as a child in the 1950s, it seemed that people were only interested in gardening in the sun. If you did have shade in the garden, you certainly did not extol it, you just quietly covered the area with ivy or pachysandra—if you were daring you might plant myrtle (periwinkle).

Fortunately, gardening trends have changed. Many wildflowers are native to woodland areas that are, by nature, shady. Even in a yard that has been sunny, you may notice that parts of the garden are plunged into shade for longer periods of the day. That is because other plants, most notably the trees, have slowly grown taller and wider over the years and are now shading previously sunny areas. Your yard has matured!

One solution to the encroaching shade would be to chop down the trees. However, ecologically and aesthetically, that is not the best choice. Instead, modify the plantings in those areas. Garden centers and mail-order catalogues carry a multitude of plants that grow successfully in the shade. Many of the gems of a shade garden would wither and die in full sun. Rejoice in the coolness of your shade.

There are three basic types of shade. Light shade implies six hours of full sun a day, or lightly dappled shade throughout the sunlight hours. Partial or half shade means less sun, usually four to six hours a day, or a heavier dappled shade during the day. Full shade is considered less than four hours of sun a day or heavily dappled sunlight all day. Thus it is not simply a matter of sun or no sun. All green plants need light to grow; sunlight is essential for the process of photosynthesis. Plants will not grow in complete darkness—all you can grow in those conditions are mushrooms.

I prefer not to call plants shade loving, rather shade tolerant. Through time, they have evolved (some plants with a little of man's genetic tinkering) to grow well in varying degrees of shade. Shade plants span the plant kingdom. Mosses are the smallest, and a good ground cover for damp, moist, deep shade—just about the toughest light and growing conditions. Look beyond the ubiquitous periwinkle (myrtle), ivy, and pachysandra for shade ground covers. Your choices are varied, from ajuga to goutweed, wild ginger to mondo grass, yellow archangel to lilyturf, winter creeper to epimedium, and more. When you think of annuals for shade, impatiens, coleus, and bedding begonias first come to mind. Broaden your horizons with evening stock, cupflower, evening primrose, flowering tobacco, pansies, and cineraria, to name a few. Myriad perennials thrive in shade—just think of all those lovely native woodland wildflowers. Japanese and wood anemones, meadowsweet, cranesbill, cardinal flower, lupine, and yellow loosestrife will brighten a light to partial shade garden for many years with little effort. Some wonderfully fragrant shrubs—witch hazel, gardenia, daphne, and sweet pepperbush—lure you into the shade to smell their flowers. Small trees, as in a woodland understory, including Cornelian cherry, silverbell, star magnolia, Japanese maple, and dogwood, rank high on my list for any shade garden.

If you can choose your shaded areas for planting, those with morning sun and afternoon shade are preferable. Early sun is less harsh, yet has the warmth to dry up morning dew, thus cutting down on fungus problems. Many plants benefit from the cooling effect of shade in the heat of the afternoon. Very dense shade can inhibit flowering of many plants. You can lighten the shade by thinning out or limbing up large trees, allowing more dappled light in.

Create the illusion of light in a shade garden by using variegated plants. The white, cream, or gold markings on plants stand out from the green, catching your eye and adding a sense of greater depth to the garden.

In summer it is about 15 degrees cooler in the shade than it is in the sun. You may find that you gravitate toward that cool woodland garden, content to weed there, even on those dog days of summer. Use your shade garden to start cool weather seeds for your fall vegetable garden. You will get much better germination and have less-stressed plants than those you try to start in full sun in summer.

Previous page: *Oak leaf hydrangea blooms in the shady garden*

Bittersweet September brings daily reminders that another gardening year is on the wane and that winter is just around the corner. For much of the country September is a "too-late" month when gardeners must enter missed planting and construction opportunities in their garden journals as reminders for the next year. But for the South and West, fall is a better "spring" than spring itself, with many days of open, cool, frost-free weather available for planting trees, shrubs, and perennials. Gardeners in Region A and Region B, however, know that spring planting of deciduous and coniferous trees, shrubs, roses, and perennials is less risky.

Regions A, B, C, D, E Set groups of potted mums and fall asters around your garden. Regrettably, in some towns, showing potted plants in front yards is an invitation to theft. Put them in the backyard.

Region A After frost has defoliated your roses, cut back the bushes to a manageable height, and before the ground freezes, mound soil over them or protect them with snow cones.

Regions B, C, D You can have woodland wildflowers around lawn trees. Mow closely, lay down several layers of newspaper, spread 3 inches of pine bark or hardwood mulch, make planting pockets through it, fill them with potting soil, and set out plants. Water at least weekly until fall rains begin.

Region D Toward the end of the month, thatch your Bermuda grass, centipede, or zoysia lawn; lime, fertilize, and spread seeds of annual ryegrass to have an apple-green turf all winter long. Sprinkle daily for two weeks to germinate the seeds.

Region E Early in the month, direct-seed fall greens and set out plants of cabbage, brussels sprouts, broccoli, and cauliflower for winter harvest. If you delay planting too long, cold weather can stall growth and set the stage for bolting (flowering) during warm spells.

Hostas line a shady garden path

HINTS, CLUES, AND ADVICE

➤ If you cannot grow lawn in an area because it is too shady and moist, consider converting it into a moss garden. You may already have some moss growing in those conditions. If so, dig up a clump, break it up, and put it in your blender with about a quart of buttermilk. Whir it for a minute and then sprinkle the liquid on the area you want to grow moss. The buttermilk seems to be a good culture base for the moss spores to grow, feeding them and keeping them moist. Place stepping-stones through the area, as moss will not take a lot of heavy traffic.

Regions A, B, C, D, E If you spend much of your day-time hours at work or commuting, using the new, safe, low-voltage night lights can boost enjoyment of your garden. A consultation with a garden lighting specialist can give you lots of ideas on the types of lights and their placement for best effect.

Region A Run a rotary mower over fallen leaves and either leave them in place or rake and pile them in a compost heap along with all the lawn clippings you can beg from neighbors. If the leaves are bone dry, wet the layers with a mild solution of dishpan detergent so the pile will not shed water.

Region A Don't feed trees and shrubs this late; the boost in growth can "tenderize" them, increasing the risk of winterkill.

Regions B, C When selecting perennials for fall planting, choose some that attract and feed butterflies and hummingbirds.

Regions C, D Look into the new complex-hybrid, cold-hardy camellias developed at the National Arboretum. They survive winters in the D.C. area—quite an achievement!

Region E If protected corners in your yard rarely seem to be bothered by frost, consider planting tropical fruit trees such as papayas, guavas, and star fruit (carambola).

Rhododendron

HINTS, CLUES, AND ADVICE

⌇ Create a shady refuge with a pergola. You can grow sun-loving plants up the columns and across the top, while shady plants thrive underneath. Don't forget that garden bench or seat, so you can relax and enjoy the view of the rest of the sunny garden.

Regions A, B, Pot up herb plants and move indoors under fluorescent lights. Spray them two or three times with insecticidal soap to rid them of insects and their eggs before bringing them inside.

Regions C, D, Plant hardy nut trees for holiday confections and to feed wildlife. Mulch around them to prevent heaving from freezing and thawing, and wrap the lower trunk loosely with hardware cloth to keep rodents from gnawing the bark. In a snow belt, it is especially important to protect all tree trunks against the gnawing of rodents that burrow beneath the snow.

Region D In the southerly reaches of Region D, especially where an ocean moderates the climate, you can plant ornamental bananas for bold foliage accents. If extreme cold threatens, wrap their trunks with several layers of spun-bonded landscape cloth for insulation. The leaves may freeze back, but new growth will come from the protected trunk.

Region E If you feel hot, dry, and dusty after a long day in your late summer garden, think of how your plants feel. But don't get carried away and try to drench them with water when the sun is burning down. Early in the morning, put on your grungy shorts and a tee shirt, attach a water wand with a 45-degree angle to a hose, and give your plants a good drenching, top and bottom. Then fill your pump sprayer with water and a bit of insecticidal soap, pump the pressure way up, and spray the top and bottom surfaces of your rose leaves. The needle-sharp spray will knock off aphids, other insects, their eggs, and fungal spores, and the insecticidal soap will disable the remainder.

Bright-flowered, shade-tolerant, variegated impatiens

HINTS, CLUES, AND ADVICE

⌁ Vegetable lovers don't despair. Although you can't grow tomatoes in shade, you can grow an abundance of salad greens, even harvest sweet lettuce in the hottest part of summer. Radishes and beets will grow in light shade, as long as the soil is friable and well drained.

Region A Empty your terra cotta containers of flowers late in the month and use the spent planter mix as a mulch. Terra cotta containers can't withstand freezing and thawing, and the physical and chemical makeup of artificial potting mixtures changes considerably after supporting plant growth for a season. You're better off buying new mixes every year.

Regions B, C When you select fruit trees for your orchard, check not only for disease resistance, but also for their "chilling hours requirement." Some cultivars are bred for long winter dormancies.

Regions C, D In protected areas, and especially on the West Coast, September is a good time for planting some of the many winter- and early spring-blooming trees and shrubs: acacias, cassias, ceanothus, and Australian plants such as Geraldton wax flower and tea plant (*Leptospermum*).

Regions D, E Set out container-grown plants of sasanqua camellia cultivars in time for them to bloom through the fall and early winter, and japonica camellias for winter and early spring color.

TIP OF THE MONTH:
Watch for fall clearances on garden tools and supplies. Stock up for the next year at reduced prices. Except in Region D, where planting goes on virtually nonstop during the winter, garden centers like to clear the decks of bulky supplies such as peat moss, planter mixes, mulches, and bagged manures to make room for Christmas merchandise.

*Blossoms of tuberous begonias brighten a
small shade garden*

HINTS, CLUES, AND ADVICE

﹏ In warm climates, light shade can be better for
plants that full sun. Plants are less likely to dry out in
the heat of the day, get scorched, or get sunburned.
Light shade gives you the widest choice of plant material—including most sun-loving plants and many plants
that are partial to more shade.

OCTOBER

Water Gardens

Any water element, whether it large or small, is a great addition to the garden. Water has a soothing effect on most people. It is easy to unwind while watching the surface of a pond. Add even a single water lily, an amazing creation of nature, and watch it open ever so slowly, petal by petal. Put in a couple of goldfish and catch the light glinting off their golden tails as they swim languidly in the pool. Gaze on the reflection of the full moon in the still water, or watch it ripple as a soft breeze kisses the water. It is quite mesmerizing.

If that sounds idealistic, perhaps it is, slightly. You will be surprised the effect any water element has on you—provided you are close enough to it to see and hear it. You can inexpensively create a water garden on a small terrace, deck, or patio with a watertight half-whiskey barrel, or you can spend thousands of dollars to have a crew come in and install a large pond, complete with stream, waterfall, lights, and plantings.

A water garden need not be naturalistic. I remember an especially striking one—a large (15 x 30 feet), light-colored brick pool, only 2 or 3 feet deep. Submerged in the water were several beautiful pots filled with aquatic plants, randomly spaced, at a distance from one another. The initial effect was somewhat stark, but it was reminiscent of a Zen meditation garden, with its carefully raked gravel and several auspiciously placed large stones.

Recently at a garden show I saw a pond kit complete with pump, wiring, preformed multilevel pool, piping, and even a little brass ornament (you could choose a frog, turtle, or fish) that sat at the edge of the pond, with water gently spilling out of its mouth. All you had to do was dig the hole, pop in the pond form, fill it with water, add plants, and plug it in.

One year, desperate to have a water feature in my own small garden, I sank a wide metal mixing bowl (about 24 inches across and 15 inches deep) near the edge of my garden, filled it with water, and dropped in a couple of water lettuces and a water hyacinth. I got such

great enjoyment out of it—as did the birds and other small wildlife that came to drink.

Birds will use your water feature for drinking and bathing only if it is not too deep for them. When you create a pond, include a very shallow area for them to enjoy. Actually, it is a good idea to have several depths to accommodate the widest range of plant material. Use the moist area at the edge of the pond to growwetland plants.

Water lilies are perhaps the showiest of the water garden plants. Hardy varieties come in a range of colors from red through pink to yellow and white. The tropical varieties may be either day- or night-blooming. The tropical ones also offer the more exotic colors—blues, purples, yellows, whites, and reds. Water lilies are usually grown in a large container, submerged to the proper depth in the water. Free-floating water hyacinths are lovely in a confined space, but have gotten out of control in some of the Southern waterways, totally clogging streams and lakes. Avoid them completely if your water feature is not totally self-contained.

Take care not to overfill a pond. A good balance in any pond is reached with a mixture of plants and creatures. In an earth-bottom pond, for every square yard (3 feet by 3 feet) of water surface, include one large water lily, two bunches of oxygenating grasses, two fish, and twelve snails. The water lily provides beauty and a visual focal point, and the lily pads also prevent loss of oxygen from the water to the air. The oxygenating grasses (often submerged and out of sight, like those in a fish tank) prevent algae formation and replace lost oxygen. Choose goldfish or koi that are at least 5 inches long to eat flies, mosquito larvae, algae, and duckweed. The snails for the pond are water snails; they will not get out and ravage your garden. In the pond they do a good job of chowing down on algae. It may take several months until a balance is reached. Then the plants and animals will be self-supporting, having happily established themselves in the pond.

One of the biggest advantages to water gardening is that, once you have designed, dug, filled it with water, and added the plants, there is little maintenance. You don't have to hoe or cultivate the plants. If you are scrupulously careful about the plants you bring in (and never let a single small two-leafed duckweed into the pond that will multiply and cover the pond with a veritable sea of plants), weeding is not a chore. And, of course, you never have to water.

Previous page: A *water garden*

Good gardeners, like the proverbial ants, plan ahead so that the first frost doesn't catch them with their plants down. After the leaves drop from deciduous trees look at the bare trees to analyze their structure. It is especially important on young trees to prune off limbs that are growing toward the trunk or that threaten to produce a weak "yoke" in the main trunk. A few trees such as maples and pines are "bleeders." That is, fall pruning will cause copious bleeding of sap. These species are customarily pruned during the summer. If you are anticipating topping a tree, don't. It is a death sentence. If you are anticipating limbing up a conifer or broad-leaved evergreen, don't. Such butchering makes them look awful. Neither grass nor ground covers will grow under them anyway, so why bother?

Regions A, B, C, D, E Begin scouting for vines and natural "collectibles" for making wreaths and swags. Northern gardeners can often find bittersweet and grape vines growing wild, while farther south trumpet creeper, honeysuckle, fox grape, and kudzu vines abound. Holly and nandina berries are seldom eaten by birds until after Christmas, and a stroll through old-growth fields or woods might yield milkweed pods, dry magnolia fruits, insect galls, osage oranges, or fruit of trifoliate oranges, depending on your climate and soil. Be sure to ask permission before you "go a'gathering."

Regions A, B Empty and bring wooden half-barrels and planter boxes indoors before a hard freeze. Freezing and thawing can destroy them.

Regions C, D Meadow voles and pine voles will eat your lily and tulip bulbs. Bait mousetraps with apple slices to trap them. Western gophers and striped ground squirrels are more difficult; you must put spring-loaded guillotine traps in their runs.

Even in Alaska this water garden flourishes in summer

HINTS, CLUES, AND ADVICE

◁ For a quick, inexpensive, in-ground water garden, dig a hole large enough to hold a wooden tub, half whiskey barrel, or even an old metal watering trough. Be sure the container has no drainage holes. You may want to line it with neoprene or heavy plastic (tough garbage can liners work well). Sink the container in the hole; fill it with water. Let the water sit for several days to allow the temperature to normalize before planting. If you have more space, sink several different sized or shaped tubs and barrels for an interesting effect.

Region A, Bring in your winter squash. Store them in a warm, dry area. They can mold in damp storage. Butternut squash will keep until late the next spring.

Regions B, C, D It's okay to leave large ornamental gourds in the garden until the outer layer is softened by frost. Bring them indoors then, and rub off the soft frozen tissue to expose the hard shell. Dry them in a warm area.

Region B Harvest tomatoes and peppers before the first frost. Tomatoes that have turned light green or pink will ripen indoors when wrapped in newspapers and stored at room temperature. Sweet peppers can be blanched and frozen; hot peppers can be dried in a microwave or oven at a very low setting. Open doors and windows and stay out of the kitchen while hot peppers are drying; their active ingredient, capsaicin, can be extremely irritating to exposed skin and eyes.

Regions D, E If you have pecan trees, start now to make harvesting the nuts easier. Set your mower quite low, scalp the grass, and rake the litter out past the drip line. You will have to mow closely and rake once or twice more, but it will make the nuts easier to see and pick up before rodents, crows, and jays steal them.

Musical falling water

HINTS, CLUES, AND ADVICE

∿ The key to a naturalistic water garden of any dimension is finishing off the edges. Create an irregular edge using large stones, laid flat. Tuck some iris or cattails amongst the stones to finish the look. If you have created a stream running into the pond, plant watercress and enjoy your own delicious greens in salads.

Regions A, B, C Plant bulbs in the garden for spring blooming. Pot up and water some, and put them in an unheated garage. Around Christmastime, bring the pots into a warm, sunny area to force them into bloom.

Regions A, B Turn on the heater in your fish pond.

Region A Wash shading paint off your greenhouse and cycle your heater. Keep a small, portable kerosene heater handy in the event of power failures that disable pilot lights on gas heaters.

Region A Prune or thin evergreens (except pines); save the boughs to use for mulching.

Region B If you are growing a wildflower meadow or prairie garden, hoe out the winter weeds now or they will continue to spread during warm spells.

Region E If you are tired of dragging hoses around the garden, now is a good time to dig ditches for new water lines to all corners of the garden. Install a master cutoff valve and two backflow check valves in tandem to prevent contamination of drinking water.

Regions C, D After a frost, bring in your tropical water lilies. Trim off and discard the tops. Store the small tubers in bags of moist potting soil. Keep them in a cool area to prevent sprouting until spring.

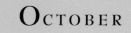

Water lilies

HINTS, CLUES, AND ADVICE

↘ Fish in a water garden are a natural mosquito control. The fish, however, may be an attractive dinner to large birds. Egrets and great blue herons are uncanny in their ability to discover prey in a new pond, or even new additions to an existing pond. Racoons are good fishermen. To protect the fish, you may have to cover the pond with bird netting. A 12- to 18-inch electric fence will keep the land predators away.

Regions A, B, C, D, E Consider large cacti or succulents for dramatic houseplants. Caution: they are a no-no around small children.

Regions A, B, C Set out herbaceous peonies for bloom in the spring. Be extremely careful with planting depth; follow directions exactly. The newer cultivars are comparatively expensive but include some rare colors and blossom types.

Regions B, C After they have bloomed, cut and save the tall, strong, fibrous stalks of swamp sunflower or Jerusalem artichoketo use as temporary stakes for flowers and small vegetables such as peas.

Regions B, C, D October is not too late to plant pansies for winter and spring color. They are unbelievably hardy. After a hard frost you will fear that they are goners, only to see them revive during the next warm spell. No other garden flower can match pansies for color during these stressful months.

Region E Take a good look at the annuals that have served you well during the summer. While they might, if spared an "arctic express," continue to bloom all winter, new, young plants of cold-tolerant species will serve you better. Grit your teeth and pull out your summertime sweethearts.

TIP OF THE MONTH:

Take a close look at your garden tools. If they are awkward or heavy, replace them with smaller, high-quality forged tools. Donate the old ones to Goodwill. Poorly designed or shoddy tools exasperate good gardeners like garbled syntax annoys grammarians. You will be amazed at how good tools ease your garden chores. Finding high-quality garden tools is going to become even more difficult as competition forces more manufacturers to use imported woods for handles, cheap rolled steel for blades, and flimsy sockets to join them. If we all stop buying this sorry merchandise, upgrading will begin. Tall gardeners note: Avoid buying short-handled tools; they were invented by short people to get revenge. You would have to be a masochist to continue using them.

Variegated Iris pallida *loves a wet site at the edge of a water garden*

HINTS, CLUES, AND ADVICE

↜ Many water plants are heavy feeders. Place soluble fertilizer tablets around the roots of the water lilies and other ornamentals at least once a month, especially if they are in a container. If they are in an unlined earthen pond, they will not need dividing, but those in containers will every few years.

↜ Tropical water lilies, for all their lush beauty, are not hardy and must remain in a completely frost-free environment. You can either treat them as disposable annuals if you live in an area with cold winters, or you can bring them inside and keep them in a semidark area, Make sure they do not dry out.

NOVEMBER

Variegation—Plants of Distinction

Variegated plants are rarely considered a group unto themselves. Yet the longer I garden, and the more I travel and see others' gardens, the more I appreciate this wide-ranging group of plants for the unique characteristic that makes them so versatile. Variegated, by definition, is "having marks, stripes, or blotches of some color other than the basic background color, in plants that are green."

As you walk into a garden, you first notice vibrant colors, pale colors, and white, especially when contrasted against green foliage. In most cases what you see are the flowers. Upon closer inspection, you discern the leaves—their varying shapes, sizes, and textures. If there is a variegated plant, you will quickly spot it. Since most leaves last longer than the flower of a plant, it is a bonus to have a plant that can stand out even without the benefit of its blooms. Variegation simply adds color to what would otherwise be a monochromatic plant.

Although the most common variegation is white or cream overlaid on green, it is by no means the only combination. Variegated foliage encompasses crimson, purple, orange, red, yellow, pink, apricot, yellow, mauve, and the varying shades and tints of green. Most plants are bicolored—with one color overlapping the basic green of the leaf. Rarer and equally choice are the tricolored and multicolored variegations. Even if these plants never set forth a flower, they would be real eye-catchers. For example, 'Chameleon' *Houttuynia* is a knockout with vibrant red stems holding up heart-shaped leaves irregularly patterned with red, green, pink, and even a touch of bronze. This creeper is a standout in a partially shaded corner of my garden.

Variegations come in as wide a range of forms as shades and tints of the colors they wear. Even the simplest type of variegation, that of contrasting leaf edging, has many variations. In this type, the margin of the leaf is often white, cream, or yellow, accenting the shape of the leaf. The edge may be delineated with a thin line or a bold swath of color. The variegation may follow the margin of the leaf with geometric precision or may be irregular. To add to the possibilities of combinations and permutations, all the variegations described may be reversed, with green as the edging and the contrasting color as the central portion of the leaf.

I find contrasting veining to be the prettiest and often the most intricate form of variegation. Here, the variegation is along the veins of the leaf, seeming to reveal the skeleton or inner structure of the leaf. On plants with small leaves, it gives a dainty, almost lacy effect. Caladiums have big heart-shaped leaves with contrasting veining often accompanied by bold splotches of color—bright red veins on deep green leaves spotted with hot pink. If you are looking for plants to colorize your shade garden, these certainly will.

Another form of variegation is contrasting stripes. Like the other types, this is broadly interpreted in nature, from faint pinstripes to bold bands of color. Usually stripes run the length of the leaf, parallel to the center vein. Canna 'Bengal Tiger' is aptly named with bold yellow stripes on the large green leaves. You can just imagine a tiger lurking behind it, waiting to pounce. This plant is especially handsome when the early morning or late afternoon sunlight catches the leaves. Zebra grass and porcupine grass both have contrasting horizontal stripes on their long leaves.

Because of their showy nature, variegated plants can be used to define the space of the other, plain-Jane green plants around them. They also lend a sense of movement to a garden. But be careful how you use them. You can get away with more subtly variegated plants, even in a naturalistic landscape, than with the more striking ones. The boldly variegated plants need special placement. Choose a spot that you want to be a focal point—the end of a path or corner of the house—and site a single prominent variegated plant there. Several different boldly variegated plants will fight with one another for attention if planted on opposite sides of a path. On the other hand, you can be daring, and make a big bold splash, planting them closely together.

Most recently I came to appreciate variegated plants for their use in evening gardens. As the sunlight fades, the green portion of the leaf gradually blends into the deepening gloom of night. The variegation, whatever its form or design, seems to float. Picture the heart-shaped outlines from hosta leaves, hovering near the ground. Pointing toward the sky are the sword-like stripes of *Iris pallida*. Floating above your head, like a hundred night moths fluttering on a breeze are the delicately outlined leaves of the 'Butterfly' Japanese maple. This is the true magic of variegated plants.

Previous page: *Japanese painted fern and Pulmonaria*

Even the gardeners who consider themselves perfectly rational human beings often suffer from a nameless apprehension during gray November. Call it "withdrawal symptoms," a longing for the splendid summertime and gorgeous autumn that so recently bathed your days. Whatever name you give the ailment, there is a cure, and the commercial growers of pot plants know it. They load stores with several kinds of flowers that will endure the hard life imposed by overly warm, desert-dry, indoor air. One of the best pot plants for lifting spirits is the 'Reiger' begonia, which somewhat resembles a jumbo version of wax begonias from the garden. It will continue blooming for weeks if you remove the foil or plastic decoration from around the pot and water only when the top 2 inches of the soil are dry.

Regions A, B, C, D, E Along with 'Reiger' begonias, potted azaleas are in season. Surprise your spouse or a special friend with one in his or her favorite color. In northern climates, potted azaleas should be considered sacrificial lambs. Even if you can bring them through the winter with TLC, they probably will not bloom again nor endure the next winter outside.

Region A Protect conifers and broad-leaved evergreens in exposed locations with burlap or snow fence screens to lessen the risk of desiccation.

Regions B, C, D If you put up owl and flicker houses now, the birds will become accustomed to them and may move in next spring. Only the small owls that nest in holes in trees will move into owl houses; the larger species prefer to build their own stick nests.

Regions C, D, E Start strawberries on raised beds covered with black plastic. Run drip irrigation tubing down each row to simplify watering.

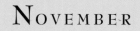

Bright tulips contrast with variegated grass

HINTS, CLUES, AND ADVICE

↝ When pairing variegated plants in the garden, look for ones that echo each other's colors without repeating the same pattern. For instance, a 'Carol Mackie' daphne, with its cream-edged, small, rounded leaves would be set off nicely by the somewhat striped leaves of the variegated Solomon's seal.

Regions B, C, D Gather the everlasting flowers, dried herbs, and decorative seed pods you prepared or collected during the summer. Assemble your ribbons, bows, pins, and glue gun, and have fun creating wreaths, swags, decoupages, and winter arrangements.

Regions A, B If deer browse your fruit trees, drive steel posts in a random pattern around the trees and string wires between them. Tie pieces of bird flasher tape to the wires as a warning. Space the wires to deny deer the takeoff run they need for jumping fences.

Regions B, C Before birds strip the plants, visit an arboretum to learn which shrubs have colorful berries and which have bark that looks good against the snow.

Region C As a variation on pecans, consider planting "hicans," which are hybrids between hickories and pecans. They have large, thin-shelled nuts with a high oil content and a unique flavor. Some hican cultivars will bear nuts where winters are too cold for pecans to do well.

Region E Plant blueberries now; you can grow them wherever the soil is acidic enough, which eliminates all the Southwest and California except for the rainy coastal plateau along its northern coast. In hot climates the rabbit-eye cultivars give the best results.

Variegated dogwoods, 'Welchii' and 'Rainbow'

HINTS, CLUES, AND ADVICE

⌁ Use variegated plants to brighten up any dark spot in the garden. The paler portions of the leaves catch and reflect any light back to your eyes. From a distance, highly contrasted variegations, such as the bright white edges on *Hosta crispula,* appear to be a bit above the leaf. Such plants draw you into the garden, perhaps because subconsciously you need to confirm what your eyes see.

Regions A, B, C, D, E Give that friend who loves flower arranging a gift certificate from a florist. Flower arrangers never seem to have enough frogs and other holders; tall, slim vases; shears, accessories, florist tape, and wire.

Regions A, B, C, D Put up bird feeders. There really are squirrel-proof designs. You need three: a roofed feeder with an overhang that will exclude snow and rain, an open tray for birds that don't like a roof over their heads, and a "thistle feeder" (actually, they are niger, not thistle, seeds) for finches and other small seed eaters such as chipping sparrows. Colorful birds can be your "flowers of the winter."

Regions D, E Now is the time to plant adapted cultivars of fruit trees, kinds that will bear fruit with relatively few chilling hours. Your nursery should have bare-root or containerized trees in stock by now. Ask your Cooperative Extension Service office for a list of adapted cultivars.

Region E There is no more efficient converter of vegetable garden and fruit orchard wastes than rabbits. Their manure makes a wonderful dressing for flower and vegetable beds. Keep them as pets: children, grandchildren, and neighbors' children will love their floppy ears and hoppy habits. Pet superstores sell ready-made rabbit pens at reasonable prices.

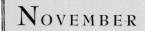

Variegated coleus show great variety

HINTS, CLUES, AND ADVICE

❧ Variegated plants add depth to a shady border. To give an illusion of a larger garden space, place plants with the least-contrasting variegations in the foreground and those with the most contrast the farthest away from where people will see them.

Regions A, B, C Your new-season seed and plant cata-
logs will be delivered soon. Grow at least a half-dozen
new (to you) kinds each season, and if you have time,
jot down notes on their performance. If they do poorly
or rate as mediocre, out with them! Make room for better plants the next year. In northern gardens you need to
make the most of every precious day of the growing season, and every square foot of your garden. If a plant
doesn't perform well, don't consider it a reflection on
your gardening skill. Consider it part of the learning
process … nothing ventured, nothing gained.

Region C Kiwi should do well in the southern half of
Region D. Remember, it takes two to tango, but one
male vine can dance with three or four females. The
small, hardy, smooth-skinned kiwis will survive **Region
B** and **Region C** winters but aren't adapted to hot climates.

Region E Many is the warm-climate gardener who real-
izes one day that "Oops! I shouldn't have planted that
tree where it would overhang the drive or walk!" Many
tropical species bear and drop fruit at a young age; shed
loads of aging leaves and limbs, or attract birds that
deposit droppings on on all and sundry. Remember to
check these points when purchasing new or replacement
trees for your yard.

TIP OF THE MONTH:

Who isn't fascinated by big pumpkins, with
Halloween still fresh in mind? You can grow them to a
whopping 200-pound size anywhere in the USA, but
the truly enormous pumpkins come from coastal climates at northern latitudes, warmed by the Gulf
Stream. The world record is around 800 pounds.
Imagine the logistics of hoisting and hauling a pump-
kin that large! If you are game to try for a big pump-
kin, you need to start with seeds of special varieties
such as 'Atlantic' that are bred for size; Jack-o'-lantern
varieties seldom grow to more than 30 pounds regard-
less of where they are grown.

Snow-on-the-mountain

HINTS, CLUES, AND ADVICE

∿ Include at least one variegated evergreen in your garden. While all evergreens are valuable for their shape and texture, a variegated evergreen is a real attention-grabber. Especially in the short, bleak days of winter when the sky and much of the garden is gray, it may be the only color in the garden. Year-round, as the sun goes down, the light portions of the leaves continue to stand out.

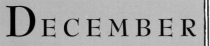

DECEMBER

Sounds from the Garden

You can easily create a garden that will dazzle all the senses. Imagine it—a beautiful place filled with colorful flowers for your eyes; sweet fragrances for your nose, soft leaves for your fingers; luscious fruits to delight your taste buds. Did you even consider sound in that garden—or just the sound of silence?

The sense of hearing may not be the primary one to consider in creating a garden, but it should not be overlooked. Think of a garden without a single sound—there is something static about it—almost as if the garden is not totally alive. Generally a garden is a tranquil place—but not silent. Natural sounds bring the picture to life, greatly adding to the pleasure you get from the garden.

If you have a woodland garden, listen for the sound of the wind murmuring through the branches of the tall pines. Even if you don't have a small woods, you can re-create the sound by planting several white pines. They are fast growing and will grace the garden with their airy sounds in several years. Walk through the woodland garden, where the layer of pine needles muffles your footsteps.

Leaves have various sound qualities in different seasons. In summer, you can tell when it is going to storm because you can see the undersides of the leaves on many trees. You also hear the leaves rustling in the gathering wind as they blow around to show you their undersides. The crackling rustle of dry leaves in an autumn wind has a sharper tone. Once the leaves fall to the ground, you rake them into big piles. Remember the sounds you made and heard as a child, running and jumping into the leaf piles?

Perhaps the quietest time in the garden is in winter, just after a snow. The air is still, the plants are covered with a thick, sound-absorbing layer of white powder, not a creature is stirring. As the sun warms the snow, you start to hear the plop of clumps of snow dropping from tree branches onto the moist, snow-laden ground.

Spring returns to the garden, and you can almost hear the plants pushing themselves out of the thawing earth. Listen to the return of birds to the garden. Their songs gently awaken you in the morning and serenade you in the evening. The deciduous trees begin to green, leafing out with leaves barely large enough to make a quiet rustle on the wind. Tree frog eggs hatch, and you hear the sounds coming from your pond or wet woodland of hundreds of peepers in the spring night.

In summer the garden is abuzz with bees collecting pollen from the flowers. Hummingbirds make a soft whirring sound as they flit from flower to flower drinking up nectar. I have often been out in my garden at night and heard the gentle whir of a sphinx moth, gathering nectar while pollinating my night-blooming plants. Summer also brings the sometimes gentle, sometimes thunderous, sound of rain.

Water is one of the best elements for sound in the garden. The Japanese truly appreciate the sounds of water, utilizing them in garden designs. You often see a hollow bamboo flume that lets water drip down into a stone basin, making a cool, lyrical sound. A wonderful use of water to create sounds is the Japanese deer scare. A hollow bamboo pipe slowly fills with water dripping from another bamboo pipe slightly above it. When the lower pipe is filled, it tips down, emptying. Lightened, it swings up and strikes a rock or piece of wood with a "clack," supposedly scaring deer away.

A small waterfall gives a rushing sound. In a stream, you can create small rapids with stones sticking their heads above the water, making a gentle burbling sound. You can make the sound more intense by adding more stones or speeding the flow of water.

Make a quiet space in your garden where you can sit, undisturbed, and enjoy all the special sounds in the garden. You will come to recognize the hoots of the owls at night, the mournful cooing of doves in the evening, and the sounds of whatever other birds and wildlife are indigenous to your area. Catch the sound of the wind—and enjoy the solace . . . if the surrounding gardeners are not making too much noise.

Previous Page: A "deer scare" in a Japanese garden

One of the many blessings that come to gardeners is that friends and family, with sufficient hints, can be persuaded to give them gardening books, videos, and garden tools for Christmas rather than clothing that isn't needed or doesn't fit. If you're looking for garden books to give, the "hot buttons" in home horticulture (the fastest-growing segments) are perennials, herbs, container gardening, water gardening, and butterfly/hummingbird gardening. When selecting books on these specialties, look among the first few pages for the copyright date and the name of the publisher, to be sure of getting recent publications written for North America by American or Canadian writers.

Regions A, B, C, D, E If you are unsure what a gardening friend would like for Christmas, give a gift certificate from your local garden center.

Regions A, B, C, D At this season of the year, when plants are dormant, you can appreciate what designers call "architectural features" in your landscape. They aren't necessarily just constructions such as arbors, fences, walls, terraces, and balustrades, but also plants with strong lines that look good against snow or a gray sky. Shrubs or trees with strong vertical or horizontal lines, tall ornamental grasses that stand above all but the deepest snows, conifers that move with the wind, berried plants with bright fruits … all add life, apparent height, or action to landscapes.

Bamboo leaves rustle in the wind

HINTS, CLUES, AND ADVICE

～ A stand of bamboo not only diminishes the level of sound reaching you from the street, but it also creates a distraction by making its own sounds when a breeze flutters the leaves. Tall ornamental grasses also serve dual purposes—privacy screens and sound-producing barriers. The wind sounds lovely rustling the long leaves.

Regions A, B, C Invest in an electrically heated dog watering dish to keep fresh water thawed for birds. During the winter they need water as often as they do food.

Regions A, B On a dry day, mush around your garden. Pull snow away from shrubs or trees, and check for rodent damage. Set traps if necessary. Your hardware store will have humane traps for rabbits, squirrels, racoons, and opossums.

Regions B, C Gardeners everywhere are rediscovering the hellebores, which include the Christmas rose and Lenten rose. These are not roses but are bell-like flowers with the incredible ability to bloom when all else is dormant. If you like the idea, make a note on your calendar to purchase plants next spring.

Regions B, C, D Sift and spread an inch or two of compost over asparagus and rhubarb beds and peony plants. These are never divided and rarely, if ever, moved. Compost gradually releases nutrients and rebuilds the vigor of old perennial plants.

Region E Cut back and wrap trunks of banana trees if they are occasionally damaged by hard freezes in your area. In the event of extremely cold weather, citrus trees can sometimes be saved by running a sprinkler on them all night. They may be coated by icicles by morning, but often will recover.

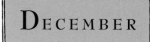

*Dripping water sounds attract birds—
and soothe the gardener*

HINTS, CLUES, AND ADVICE

A suburban garden can be a cacophony of sounds, especially if you live on a busy street. A solid wood fence acts as a partial sound barrier, keeping the street sounds from your backyard oasis. A thick evergreen hedge also muffles sounds.

Regions A, B, C, D, E Sharpen your hoes, spades, mattocks, and posthole diggers. Use a file rather than a grinding wheel, which tends to overheat steel and to remove more metal than is necessary to hone a cutting edge. For the sake of safety, grip tools in a vise when sharpening and wear leather gloves.

Regions A, B Protect small yew or hemlock shrubs with burlap stretched around stakes.

Regions C, D, E Save worn blankets to protect tender plants against frost. They protect plants much better than plastic and are less likely to blow away.

Region D Ask your garden center for the shrub named *loropetalum*. The cultivar 'Burgundy' blooms for several weeks and the foliage turns bronze in the fall.

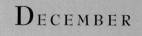

Running water rushing over stones

HINTS, CLUES, AND ADVICE

⌁ For a small waterfall in a pond to be at all musical, it is necessary to have a good dripstone. The dripstone needs to extend far enough forward to form a sound chamber between itself and the water. Water should drop, not slide, from the lip. It can take a lot of patience to carve a dripstone just right, but you'll know exactly when you've done it—the sound will be perfect.

Regions A, B, C, D As heartless as it may seem, you may have to call the animal control center if feral cats lurk around your bird feeder. One cat running wild can consume more than 200 wild birds per year. You can rationalize the depredations of native predators such as the few species of hawks that kill and eat birds, but feral cats are growing in number and are significantly reducing the bird count, particularly of groundfeeding species.

Regions C, D This may be the December you lose your rosemary, even the most hardy cultivars such as 'Arp' and 'Salem'. Rosemary is evergreen and continues to grow during warm fall days. The plants need a hardening-off period of gradually colder days and nights. Without it, a sudden drop of 40 or 50 degrees F. can be disastrous. If a "blue norther" or "arctic express" comes thundering south, it can wipe out your rosemary overnight. It might help, though, to cover your plants with a blanket.

Region E Have you tried the new colors in caladiums and bromeliads? It would be hard to find more beautiful plants for light to moderate shade. Their variegated foliage illuminates dark corners, and the bromeliads bring a bonus of fantastic blooms.

TIPS OF THE MONTH:

Resolve now to grow, rather than buy, next year's Christmas gifts for special friends. Rosemary plants can be trained into miniature Christmas trees, and creeping fig can cover fanciful animal topiaries stuffed with sphagamum moss.

Most TV gardening programs have traditionally appeared on public television stations. Some such as The Victory Garden have been aired for nearly 20 years. Now, the expanding interest in home gardening is attracting programs on cable television as well. At least one home garden TV network will be on line in 1996 broadcasting a great variety of programs on gardening and landscaping. Between your old favorites on PBS and the new features on cable, the opportunities for learning and wholesome entertainment will be immense.

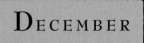

*The wind sighs through evergreens
in winter*

HINTS, CLUES, AND ADVICE

 Catch the sound of the wind with wind chimes.
They can be made from many materials, most commonly
metal and ceramic. Hang breakable chimes in a sheltered
location, or the first big storm will destroy them. The
pitch of the chimes varies from deep resounding notes to
a high tinkle. Try the wind chimes in the store before
you buy them to be sure they have an appealing sound.
To get the most realistic sound, blow on them rather
than knocking them together with your finger.

APPENDIX

JANUARY
Lightening the Load—Lowering Garden Maintenance

MULCHES
*Bark, shredded or finely chopped
Black plastic
*Buckwheat hulls
Builder's sand
Cardboard (pictured below)
Clay pot shards
*Cocoa hulls
*Coffee grounds
*Compost, well-rotted
*Corn cobs or stalks, ground
*Cottonseed hulls
*Leaves, shredded or chopped
*Grass clippings (add no more than 1 inch at a time)
Gravel
*Hay
Landscape cloth
*Manure, well-rotted
Marbles
*Newspaper, finely shredded (do not use colored sections)
*Nut shells
*Paper, finely shredded (use white paper with black ink only,
    no glossy paper or colors)
*Peanut shells
*Pine needles
*Salt hay
*Sawdust
*Seaweed
Stones
*Straw
*Sugar cane, shredded
*Wood chips (pictured at right)

* These are organic and will break down over time, enriching
    the soil.

Previous Page: *Cutleaf maple in the snow*

INTERPLANTING
Daffodils with daylilies
Sweet violets with hostas
Tulips with forget-me-nots
Early spring bulbs (crocus, Greek windflower) in ivy
Corn with melons
Pole beans with corn
Tomatoes with basil
Eggplant or peppers with lettuce
Spring bulbs (daffodils, tulips) with pansies

Cardboard (above) with woodchips (below)

FEBRUARY
Fragrance—The Aromatic Garden

FRAGRANT FLOWERS

Angel's trumpet, *Brugmansia sp., Datura sp.*
Autumn clematis, *Clematis paniculata*
Candytuft, *Iberis sempervirens*
Carolina jasmine, *Gelsemium sempervirens*
Chilean jasmine, *Mandevilla suaveolens (M. laxa)*
Citrus (lemon, orange, etc.), *Citrus sp.*
Clove pink, carnation, *Dianthus sp.*
Common wallflower, *Cheiranthus cheiri*
Crocus, *Crocus sp.*
Cymbidium orchid, *Cymbidium sp.*
Daffodil, *Narcissus sp.*
Daphne, *Daphne sp.*
Elder, *Sambucus sp.*
Evening primrose, *Oenothera sp.*
Flowering tobacco, *Nicotiana sp.*
Four o'clock, *Mirabilis jalapa*
Freesia, *Freesia refracta*
Gardenia, *Gardenia sp.*
Grape hyacinth, *Muscari botryoides*
Heliotrope, *Heliotropium arborescens*
Honeysuckle, *Lonicera sp.*
Hyacinth, *Hyacinthus sp.*
Jasmine, *Jasminum sp.*
Lilac, *Syringa sp.*
Lilies, *Lilium sp.*
Lily-of-the-valley, *Convallaria majalis*

Magnolia, *Magnolia sp.*
Mignonette, *Reseda odorata*
Mock orange, *Philadelphus coronarius*
Night-flowering jessamine, *Cestrum nocturnum*
Oregon grape holly, *Mahonia aquifolium*
Peony, *Paeonia sp.*
Queen of the night, *Selenicereus grandiflorus*
Roses, *Rosa sp.*
Scented bouvardia, *Bouvardia longiflora*
Star jasmine, *Trachelospermum jasminoides*
Stephanotis, *Stephanotis floribunda*
Stock, *Matthiola sp.*
Summer hyacinth, *Galtonia candicans*
Sweet alyssum, *Lobularia maritima*
Sweet olive, *Osmanthus fragrans (pictured at left)*
Sweet pea, *Lathyrus odoratus*
Sweet rocket, *Hesperis matronalis*
Sweet violet, *Viola odorata*
Tuberose, *Polyanthes tuberosa*
Viburnum, *Viburnum carlesii, V. x burkwoodii*
Water lily, *Nymphaea odorata*
Wattle (Mimosa), *Acacia sp.*
Wisteria, *Wisteria sp.*
Witch hazel, *Hamamelis sp.*

Sweet olive

FRAGRANT FOLIAGE

Anise hyssop, *Agastache foeniculum*
Basil, *Ocimum basilicum*
Bay (sweet bay), *Laurus nobilis*
Bergamot (oswego tea, bee balm), *Monarda didyma*
Borage, *Borago officinalis*
Boxwood, *Buxus sp.*
Calamint, *Calamintha neptoides (C. nepeta nepeta)*
Catnip, *Nepeta sp.*
Chamomile, *Anthemis nobilis*
Chervil, *Anthriscus cerefolium*
Coriander, *Coriandrum sativum*
Dill, *Anethum graveolens*
Eucalyptus, *Eucalyptus sp.*
Fennel, *Foeniculum vulgare*
Lavender, *Lavandula sp.*
Lemon balm, *Melissa officinalis*

Lemon grass, *Cymbopogon citratus*
Lemon verbena, *Lippia citriodora*
Marjoram, *Origanum majorana*
Mint, *Mentha sp.*
Pennyroyal, *Mentha pulegium*
Rosemary, *Rosmarinus officinalis*
Sage, *Salvia officinalis*
Scented geraniums, *Pelargonium graveolens,*
    P. crispum, and others
Sweet flag, *Acorus sp.*
Sweet woodruff, *Galium odoratum*
Tansy, *Tanacetum vulgare*
Tarragon, *Artemisia dracunculus*
Thyme, *Thymus sp.*
Wormwood, *Artemisia absinthium*
Yarrow, *Achillea sp.*

Dill, thyme, parsley

MARCH
Beautiful Food—Using Fruits, Vegetables, and Herbs in the Landscape

EDIBLES WITH COLORFUL FLOWERS

Amaranth	green, purple, red	Jerusalem artichoke	yellow
Artichoke	lavender	Nasturtium	orange, red, yellow,
Beans	red, purple, white		salmon, burgundy
Cardoon	lavender	Okra	white, yellow
Chives	lavender, white	Peas	purple, white
Dill	greenish yellow with an	Rosemary	pale blue, pink, white
	attractive umbel form	Salsify	blue
Eggplant	lavender	Thyme	pink, white, purple
Garlic	white		

LEAF COLOR—The color of the leaves can be used as a palette when designing the garden.

Gray to bluish leaves	Pinks and reds	Yellow to light green	Variegated leaves
Artichoke	Beets	Carrots	White ornamental kale
Cabbage	Opal basil	Endive	Variegated lemon balm
Cardoon	Red cabbage	Nasturtiums	Nasturtium 'Alaska'
Kale	Red chard	Lemon thyme	Tricolor sage
Lavender	Pink cress		Society garlic
Leeks	Purple ornamental kale		Gold-edged thyme
Marjoram	Red lettuces		
Onion	Purple mustard		
Rosemary	Purple sage		

FRAGRANT LEAVES

Basil	Fennel	Parsley	Tomato
Chamomile	Mint	Sage	Thyme
Chives	Oregano	Strawberry	

ESOTERIC EDIBLE PARTS

Artichokes	Immature flowers
Amaranth	Leaves ('Love Lies Bleeding', 'Red Stripe Leaf', 'Early Splendor')
Anise hyssop	Leaves and flowers
Balloon flower (Platycodon)	Immature leaves
Love-in-a-mist (Nigella sp.)	Seeds
Nasturtium	Leaves and flowers
Violet	Leaves and flowers

Peppers

COLORFUL VEGETABLES

Beans	Yellow, green, purple
Cucumber	Yellow, green
Eggplant	Purple, white, yellow, purple & white
Peppers (pictured at right)	Green, brown, violet, purple, red, yellow, orange
Squash	Yellow, green, orange, green & white
Tomatoes	Red, orange, yellow, white, green, striped

APRIL
Controlling Wildlife in the Garden

COMPANION PLANTING
Attractant Crops—Attract Beneficial Insects

Caraway
Catnip
Daisy
Dill
Fennel
Hyssop
Lemon balm
Lovage
Mint
Parsley
Rosemary
Thyme
Yarrow

Lacewing

Repellant Crops—Keep Certain Pests Away

Catnip	Repels green peach aphids and squash bugs
Radish	Repels cucumber beetles from cucumber and squash
Southernwood	Repels flea beetles from plants in cabbage family
Tansy	Repels green peach aphids and squash bugs
Wormwood	Repels flea beetles from plants in cabbage family

BENEFICIAL ANIMALS

Bats	Little brown bat eats moths, caddis flies, midges, beetles, and mosquitos
Birds	Flycatchers, swallows, warblers, nuthatches and others consume a large number of insects.
Snakes	Garter snake, eastern ribbon snake, western terrestrial garter snake, green snake, grass snake, and brown snake eat slugs, snails, and insects Corn snake, black rat snake, and milk snake eat mice and rats
Spiders	Eats wide variety of insects caught in web

BENEFICIAL INSECTS

Aphid midges	Aphid predators
Bees	Pollinators
Dragonflies	Eat mosquitoes, gnats, and midges
Fireflies	Eat insect larvae, slugs, and snails
Ground beetles	Night feeders prey on cabbage root maggots, cutworms, snail and slug eggs, armyworms, and tent caterpillars
Hister beetles	Eat insect larvae, slugs, and snails
Lacewings	Prey on aphids, scale insects, small caterpillars, and thrips (*pictured above*)
Lady beetles	Feed on aphids, mealybugs, and spidermites—both adults and larvae eat pests
Parasitic wasps	Trichogramma, chalcids, braconids, ichneumonids control whiteflies, aphids, and some caterpillars
Praying mantis	Indiscriminant eaters of many types of insects—both pests and allies.
Rove beetles	Decompose manure and plant material; others eat root maggots
Syrphid flies	Lay eggs in aphid colonies; larvae eat aphids
Tachinid flies	Lay eggs on cutworms, caterpillars, corn borers, and stinkbugs
Tiger beetles	Eat insect larvae, slugs, and snails
Yellow jackets	Feed flies, caterpillars, and larvae to their brood

MAY
Color & Texture for Contrast

WHITE FLOWERS
Baby's breath, *Gypsophila sp.*
Bear's breeches, *Acanthus sp.*
Candytuft, *Iberis sp.*
Honesty, *Lunaria annua (seed pods)*
Lily-of-the-valley, *Convallaria majalis*
Pampas grass, *Cortaderia selloana*
Solomon's seal, *Polygonatum sp.*

YELLOW FLOWERS
Coneflower, *Rudbeckia sp.*
Coreopsis, *Coreopsis sp.*
Daffodil, *Narcissus sp.*
Eleclampane, *Inula sp.*
Globeflower, *Trollius sp.*
Goldenrod, *Solidago sp.*
Heliopsis, *Heliopsis scabra*
Leopard's bane, *Doronicum sp.*
Ox-eye chamomile, *Anthemis tinctoria*
Sneezeweed, *Helenium autumnale*
Verbascum, *Verbascum sp.*
Yarrow, *Achillea sp.*

GREEN FLOWERS OR BRACTS
Bells of Ireland, *Molucella laevis*
Euphorbia, *Euphorbia sp.*
Stinking hellebore, *Helleborus foetidus*

BLUE FLOWERS
Balloon flower, *Platycodon grandiflorum*
Bellflower, *Campanula sp.*
Catmint, *Nepeta sp.*
Cupid's dart, *Catanache caerulea*
Forget-me-not, *Myosotis sp.*
Globe thistle, *Echinops sp.*
Larkspur, *Delphinium sp.*
Lily-of-the-Nile, *Agapanthus sp.*
Love-in-a-mist, *Nigella damascena*
Monkshood, *Aconitum sp.*
Pincushion flower, *Scabiosa sp.*
Quamash, *Camassia sp.*
Sea holly, *Eryngium sp.*
Speedwell, *Veronica sp.*

VIOLET FLOWERS
Gay feather, *Liatris sp.*
Heliotrope, *Heliotropium (pictured at right)*
Lythrum, *Lythrum sp.*
Meadow rue, *Thalictrum sp.*
Plantain lily, *Hosta sp*
Sage, *Salvia sp.*

RED FLOWERS (Includes tints of pink)
Astilbe, *Astilbe sp.*
Avens, *Geum chiloense*
Bearded tongue, *Penstemon sp.*
Bee balm (Oswego tea), *Monarda didyma*
Bleeding heart, *Dicentra sp.*
Campion, *Lychnis sp.*
Clarkia, *Clarkia sp.*
Coral bells, *Heuchera sp.*
Crocosmia, *Crocosmia sp.*
Fleabane, *Erigeron sp.*
Incarvillea, *Incarvillea sp.*
Love-lies-bleeding, *Amaranthus caudatus*
Mallow, *Lavatera trimestris*
Nerine, *Nerine bowdenii*
Obedient plant, *Physotegia virginiana*
Peony, *Paeonia sp.*
Pinks, *Dianthus sp.*
Saxifrage, *Saxifraga sp.*
Sea pink, *Armeria maritima*
Siberian tea, *Bergenia cordata*

ORANGE FLOWERS
Blanket flower, *Gaillardia grandiflora (G. Aristata)*
Calendula (pot marigold), *Calendula officinalis*
Chinese lantern, *Physalis franchetii*
Gazania, *Gazania x hybrida*
Marigold, *Tagetes sp.*
Red hot poker, *Kniphofia sp.*

Heliotrope and dusty miller

JUNE
Vertical Gardens—Growing Up

VERTICAL EDIBLES

Blackberries, *Rubus sp.*
Chinese yam, *Discorea Batatas*
Cucumbers, *Cucumis sativis*
Gourds, *Curcubita pepo*
Grapes, *Vitis sp.*
Hardy kiwi, *Actinidia*
Malabar spinach, *Basella malabar*
Maypop, *Passiflora incarnata*
Melons, *Cucumis melo*

Passionflower, *Passiflora edulus*
Peas, *Pisum sativum*
Pole beans, *Phaseolus vulgaris*
Pumpkins, *Curcubita pepo*
Raspberries, *Rubus sp.*
Scarlet runner beans, *Phaseolus coccineus* (pictured below)
Squash, *Curcubita sp.*
Sweet potatoes, *Ipomoea Batatas*
Tomatoes, *Lycopersicon lycopersicum*

VERTICAL ORNAMENTALS

Allamanda, *Allamanda sp.*
Balloon vine (Love-in-a-puff), *Cardiospermum Halicacabum*
Bittersweet, *Celastrus scandens*
Black-eyed Susan vine, *Thunbergia alata*
Blue clock vine, *Thunbergia grandiflora*
Boston ivy, *Parthenocissus tricuspidata*
Bougainvillea, *Bougainvillea sp.*
Canary creeper, *Tropaeolum peregrinum*
Carolina jasmine, *Gelsemium sempervirens*
Clematis, *Clematis sp.*
Climbing hydrangea, *Hydrangea anomala subsp. petiolaris*
Climbing nasturtium, *Tropaeolum majus*
Climbing roses, *Rosa sp.*
Creeping fig, *Ficus pumila*
Creeping gloxinia, *Asarina erubescens*
Cup-and-saucer vine (cathedral bells), *Cobaea scandens*
Cypress vine, *Ipomoea Quamoclit*
Dutchman's pipe, *Aristolochia durior*
Five-leaf akebia, *Akebia quinata*
Glory bower, *Clerodendrum sp.*
Grape ivy, *Cissus sp.*
Hops, *Humulus sp.*
Ivy, *Hedera sp.*
Jasmine, *Jasminum sp.*
Honeysuckle, *Lonicera sp.*
Hyacinth bean, *Dolichos lablab*
Kudzu, *Pueraria lobata*
Madagascar jasmine, *Stephanotis floribunda*
Mandevilla, *Mandevilla splendens*
Moonflower, *Ipomoea alba*
Moonseed, *Cocculus sp.*
Morning glory, *Ipomoea sp.*
Nasturtium, *Tropaeolum sp.*
Passionflower, *Passiflora sp.*
Porcelain berry, *Ampelopsis sp.*
Silver lace vine, *Polygonum Aubertii*
Silver vine, *Actinidia polygama*
Star jasmine, *Trachelospermum jasminoides*
Sweet pea, *Lathyrus odoratus*

Trumpet creeper/vine, *Campsis radicans*
Twining firecracker (Brazilian firecracker), *Manettia sp.*
Virginia creeper, *Parthenocissus quinequefolia*
Wax plant, *Hoya sp.*
Wild cucumber vine, *Cucumis Anguria*
Winter creeper, *Euonymus radicans*
Wisteria, *Wisteria sp.*

Scarlet runner beans

July
Edible Flowers for Beauty and Flavor

EDIBLE FLOWERS

Common name, *Botanic name*	Color	Flavor
Anise hyssop, *Agastache foeniculum*	Mauve	Licorice
Apple, *Malus sp.,*	White to light pink	Mild floral
Arugula (rocket), *Eruca Vesicaria*	Off-white	Spicy, peppery
Basil, *Ocimum basilicum,*	White to mauve	Herbal
Bee balm, *Monarda didyma*	Red	Sweet, hot minty
Borage, *Borago officinalis*	Blue	Cucumber, herbal
Broccoli, *Brassica sp.*	Yellow	Spicy
Calendula (pot marigold), *Calendula officinalis*	Yellow or orange	Mild vegetal. Used for color in cooking
Chamomile , *Anthemis nobilis*	White with yellow	Center sweet, apple
Chicory, *Cicorium intybus*	Blue	Mildly bitter
Chives, *Allium schoenoprasum*	Mauve	Oniony
Chrysanthemum, *Dendranthema sp. (Chrysanthemum sp.)*	All colors	Variable, bitter
Clove pink, *Dianthus sp.*	White, pink, or red	Floral spicy (clovelike)
Coriander (cilantro), *Coriandrum sativum*	White	Herbal
Dandelion, *Tarxacum officinale*	Yellow	Slightly sweet
Daylily, *Hemerocallis sp.*	Yellow, red, or orange	Mild vegetal, sweet
Dill , *Anethum graveolens*	Yellow	Herbal
Elderberry, *Sambucus canadensis & S. caerula*	Off-white	Sweet
English daisy, *Bellis perennis*	White and/or pink	Slightly bitter
Fennel, *Foeniculum vulgare*	Yellow	Anise
Fireweed, *Epilobium angustifolium*	Pink to mauve	Spicy
Garlic chives, *Allium tuberosum*	White	Oniony-garlic
Greek oregano, *Origanum heracleoticum*	White	Strongly herbal
Hibiscus, *Hibiscus sinensis*	Red	Mild, citrus
Honeysuckle, *Lonicera japonica*	White and yellow	Floral, sweet
Hyssop, *Hyssopus officinalis*	Blue or pink	Strongly herbal
Jasmine, *Jasminum officinale*	White	Slightly sweet
Johnny jump-up, *Viola tricolor*	Purple, white, and yellow	Mild peppermint
Lavender, *Lavandula sp. (pictured succeeding page)*	Purple	Perfumed
Lemon, *Citrus limon*	White	Citrus, sweet
Lilac, *Syringa sp.*	Lilac to white	Floral, grassy
Linden (lime, basswood), *Tilia sp.*	Off-white	Sweet
Mallow (marsh mallow), *Althaea officinalis*	Pink	Mild
Marigold, *Tagetes tenuifolia*	Yellow or orange	Citrus, tarragon (esp. 'Lemon Gem', 'Tangerine Gem')
Mint, *Mentha sp.*	White to lavender	Minty, sweet
Mustard, *Brassica sp.*	Yellow	Spicy
Nasturtium, *Tropaeolum majus (pictured succeeding page)*	Yellow, red, or orange	Spicy, peppery
Nodding onion, *Allium cernuum*	Pink	Oniony
Ocotillo, *Fouquieria splendens*	Red	Sweet, for beverage
Okra, *Abelmoschus aesculentus*	Yellow	Mild
Orange, *Citrus sinensis*	White	Sweet
Oregano, *Origanum vulgare*	White to pink	Herbal
Pansy, *Viola x wittrockiana*	All and mixed	Mild to wintergreen
Pea (garden), *Pisum sativum*	White to lavender	Floral, pea-like
Pineapple guava, *Feijoa Sellowiana*	Cream with fuchsia	Floral, delicious
Pineapple sage, *Salvia elegans*	Red	Sweet, herbal

JULY
Edible Flowers for Beauty and Flavor *(continued)*

Common name, *Botanic name*	Color	Flavor
Rose, *Rosa sp.*	All but blue	Mild floral, varies
Roselle, *Hibiscus Sabdariffa*	Yellow	Sweet, cranberry flavor
Rosemary, *Rosmarinus officinalis*	Pale blue	Herbal
Rose of Sharon, *Hibiscus syriacus*	All	Mild, slightly nutty
Runner bean, *Phaseolus coccineus*	Red-orange, and white	Beany, floral
Safflower, *Carthamus tinctorius*	Orange to red	Bitter
Sage, *Salvia officinalis*	Blue to purple	Herbal, varies
Scented geranium, *Pelargonium sp.*	Pink, red, and white	Floral, variable
Shungiku, *Chrysanthemum coronarium*	Yellow with white	Mildly bitter
Society garlic, *Tulbaghia violacea*	Pink	Oniony-garlic
Squash blossoms, *Curcubita pepo sp.*	Yellow	Mild vegetal
Summer savory, *Satureja hortensis*	Pink	Spicy
Sunflower, *Helianthus annuus*	Yellow	Bitter
Sweet marjoram, *Origanum majorana, O. vulgare*	Pink to lavender	Herbal
Sweet woodruff, *Galium odoratum*	White	Sweet, vanilla, hay
Thyme, *Thymus sp.*	White to pink	Herbal, varies
Tuberous begonia, *Begonia x tuberhybrida*	Bright, all but blue	Citrusy
Tulip, *Tulipa sp.*	All colors	Bean- or pea-like
Violet, *Viola odorata*	Violet to white	Mild perfume
Winter savory, *Satureja montana*	White	Herbal
Yucca, *Yucca sp.*	White	Sweet, mild vegetal

Lavender and nasturtium

AUGUST
Plants for an Evening Garden

SCULPTURE & SILHOUETTE

Bamboo, *Bambusa sp., Phyllostachys sp., Fargesia sp., etc.*
Cacti, *Echinocactus sp., Opuntia sp., etc.*
Corkscrew willow, *Salix Matsudana 'Tortuosa'*
Cycad (sago palm), *Cycas revoluta*
Conifers, *Chamaecyparis sp., Picea sp., Pinus sp., etc.*
Ferns, *Osmunda sp., Adiantum sp., Polystichum sp., etc.*
Harry Lauder's walking stick, *Corylus avellana 'Contorta'*
Japanese maple, *Acer palmatum, A. japonicum*
Ornamental grasses, *Cortaderia sp., Miscanthus sp., Ovina sp., etc.*
Palms, *Phoenix sp., Washingtonia sp., Chamaerops sp., etc.*
Sweet flag, *Acorus sp.*
Yucca, *Yucca sp.*

INTERESTING BARK

Canoe birch, *Betula papyrifera*
Eucalyptus, *Eucalyptus sp.*
Paperbark maple, *Acer griseum*
Red-barked dogwood, *Cornus alba*
River birch, *Betula nigra*
Striped maple, *Acer pensylvanicum*
Yellow-twig dogwood, *Cornus sericea (stolonifera) 'Flaviramea'*

FLOWERS AGLOW AT SUNSET

Bee balm, *Monarda didyma*
Cardinal flower, *Lobelia cardinalis*
Cineraria, *Senecio x hybridus*
Clematis, *Clematis sp.*
Coleus, *Coleus x hybridus*
Glory-of-the-snow, *Chionodoxa luciliae*
Grape hyacinth, *Muscari botryoides*
Japanese blood grass, *Imperata cylindrica 'Red Baron'*
Peach-leaved bellflower, *Campanula persicifolia*
Petunia, *Petunia x hybrida*
Pink turtlehead, *Chelone lyonii (C. obliqua)*
Rose daphne, *Daphne cneorum*
Shirley poppy, *Papaver rhoeas*

BRIGHT FLOWERS

Black-eyed Susan, *Rudbeckia sp.*
Canna, *Canna x generalis*
Coreopsis 'Moonbeam', *Coreopsis verticillata 'Moonbeam'*
Daffodils, *Narcissus sp.*
Exbury hybrid azaleas, *Rhododendron cv.*
Leopard's bane, *Doronicum cordatum*
Lilies, *Lilium sp.*
Marigolds, *Tagetes sp.*
Periwinkle, *Vinca minor*
Red hot poker, *Kniphofia uvaria*
Rhododendron, *Rhododendron*

Statice, *Limonium sinuatum*
Sweet sultan 'Dairy Maid', *Centaurea moschata sp. suaveolens (Amberboa moschata)*
Tulip, *Tulipa sp.*
Zinnia, *Zinnia linearis (Z. angustifolium)*

WHITE FLOWERS

Baby's breath, *Gypsophila paniculata*
Begonia, *Begonia x hybrida*
Calla lily, *Zantedeschia aethiopica*
Candytuft, *Iberis sempervirens*
Chrysanthemum, *Dendranthema sp. (Chrysanthemum sp.)*
Columbine, *Aquilegia sp.*
Deutzia, *Deutzia gracilis*
Dogwood, *Cornus florida, C. Kousa*
Dove tree (handkerchief tree), *Davidia involucrata*
Foam flower, *Tiarella cordifolia*
Fothergilla, *Fothergilla sp.*
Gaura, *Gaura Lindheimeri*
Goatsbeard, *Aruncus dioicus*
Gooseneck loosestrife, *Lysimachia clethroides*
Guinea-hen flower (checkered lily), *Fritillaria meleagris*
Heather, *Erica herbacea (E. carnea)*
Impatiens, *Impatiens sp.*
Kamchatka bugbane, *Cimicifuga simplex*
Shasta daisy, *Chrysanthemum sp.*
Shooting star, *Dodecatheon meadia*
Snapdragon, *Antirrhinum majus*
Snow-in-summer, *Cerastium tomentosum*
Snowdrops, *Galanthus nivalis*
Spirea, *Spiraea sp.*
Star magnolia, *Magnolia stellata*
Stewartia, *Stewartia sp.*
Sweet alyssum, *Lobularia maritima*
Sweet woodruff, *Galium odoratum (Asperula odorata)*
Virginia sweet spire, *Itea virginica*
White rose, *Rosa sp.*

FLOWERS FRAGRANT AT NIGHT

Coffee, *Coffea arabica*
Daphne 'Carol Mackie', *Daphne x burkwoodii 'Carol Mackie'*
Gardenia, *Gardenia jasminoides*
Gladiolus tristis, *Gladiolus tristis*
Holly osmanthus, *Osmanthus heterophyllus*
Honeysuckle, *Lonicera sp.*
Jasmine, *Jasminum sambac*
Kahili ginger, *Hedychium gardneranum*
Lemon and orange (citrus), *Citrus sp.*
Lilac, *Syringa sp.*
Lily-of-the-valley, *Convallaria majalis*
Linden, *Tilia sp.*

AUGUST
Plants for an Evening Garden *(continued)*

Mignonette, *Reseda odorata*
Moonflower, *Ipomoea alba*
Nicotiana (flowering tobacco), *Nicotiana sp.*
Oleander, *Nerium oleander*
Peruvian daffodil, *Hymenocallis narcissiflora*
Phlox, *Phlox sp.*
Russian olive, *Eleagnus angustifolia*
Stock, *Mattholia sp.*
Sweet pea, *Lathyrus odoratus*
Sweet violet, *Viola odorata*
Sweet woodruff, *Galium odoratum*
Tuberose, *Polianthes tuberosa*

NIGHT-BLOOMING PLANTS
Brugmansia (angel's trumpet), *Brugmansia sp.*
Datura (angel's trumpet), *Datura sp.*
Daylily, *Hemerocallis sp.*
Epiphyllum, *Epiphyllum oxypetalum*
Evening primrose, *Oenothera sp.*
Four o'clock (marvel of Peru), *Mirabilis jalapa*
Monvillea, *Monvillea sp.*
Moon cereus, *Selenicereus sp.*
Moonflower, *Ipomoea alba*
Nicotiana (flowering tobacco), *Nicotiana sp.*
Night-blooming cereus, *Hylocereus undatus, Nyctocereus sp.*
Night-flowering jessamine, *Cestrum nocturnum*
Night phlox, *Zaluzianskya capensis (Nycterinia capensis)*
Old man cactus, *Cephalocereus senilis*
Organpipe cactus, *Lemaireocereus Thurberi*
Saguaro, *Carnegiea gigantea*

SILVER FOLIAGE PLANTS
Artichoke, *Cynara scolymus*
Blue fescue, *Festuca ovina*
Cardoon, *Cynara cardunculus*
Dusty miller, *Senecio cineraria*
Lamb's ears, *Stachys byzantina*
Lavender, *Lavandula sp.*
Lavender cotton, *Santolina chamaecyparissus (S. incana)*
Mountain mint, *Pycnanthemum sp.*
Russian sage, *Perovskia atriplicifolia*
Sage, *Salvia officinalis*
Silver mound artemisia, *Artemisia Schmidtiana 'Silver Mound'*

VARIEGATED FOLIAGE
Bishop's weed (goutweed), *Aegpodium podagraria 'Variegatum'*
Caladium, *Caladium x hortulanum*
Dwarf whitestripe bamboo, *Pleioblastus variegatus*
Flowering kale, *Brassica oleracea—Acephala group*
Gold hakonechloa, *Hakonechloa macra aureola*
Hosta (plantain lily, funkia), *Hosta sp.*

Japanese painted fern, *Athyrium nipponicum 'Pictum'*
Lungwort, *Pulmonaria sp.*
Ornamental grasses, *Miscanthus sp. and others*
Ribbon grass (gardener's garters), *Phalaris arundinacea picta*
Snow-on-the-mountain, *Euphorbia marginata*
Variegated Italian arum, *Arum italicum 'Pictum'*
Variegated ivy, *Hedera sp.*
Variegated lilyturf, *Liriope sp.*
Yellow archangel, *Lamiastrum galeobdolon*

CLIMBERS
Clematis, *Clematis sp.*
Climbing roses, *Rosa sp.*
Honeysuckle, *Lonicera japonica*
Moonflower, *Ipomoea alba*
Variegated five-leafed akebia, *Akebia quinata variegata*
Wisteria, *Wisteria sp. (pictured below)*

FAVORITES FOR THE
EVENING GARDEN
Angel's trumpet, *Datura & Brugmansia sp.*
Artichoke, *Cynara scolymus*
Daphne 'Carol Mackie', *Daphne x burkwoodii 'Carol Mackie'*
Flowering tobacco and nicotiana, *Nicotiana sp.*
Garlic chives, *Allium tuberosum*
Heliotrope, *Heliotropium arborescens*
Hosta, *Hosta sp.*
Lamb's ears, *Stachys byzantina*
Moonflower, *Ipomoea alba*
Night-blooming cereus, *Cereus peruvianus*
Snow-on-the-mountain, *Euphorbia marginata*
Stock, *Mattholia bicornus*
Summer hyacinth, *Galtonia candicans*
Tropical water lilies, *Nymphaea sp.*
Tuberose, *Polianthes tuberosa*

White wisteria

SEPTEMBER
Shade—An Asset in the Landscape

PERENNIALS FOR SHADE

Common name, *Botanic name*	Flower color	Time of bloom
◑ Amur adonis, *Adonis amurensis*	Yellow	Early spring
◑ Astilbe, *Astilbe sp.*	Pink, white, and red	Early to late summer
◑ ● Baneberry, *Actaea sp.*	White	Late spring
◑ Barrenwort, *Epimedium sp.*	Yellow, white, pink, and red	Spring
◑ Bellflower, *Campanula sp.*	Blue to white	Early summer
◑ Bergenia, *Bergenia sp.*	Purple, white, pink, and red	Early spring
◑ Bleeding heart, *Dicentra spectabilis*	Pink and white	Mid spring to summer
◑ Bugleweed, *Ajuga reptans*	Blue to purple	Mid spring
◑ Columbine, *Aquilegia sp.*	Multi	Late spring
◑ Coral bells, *Heuchera sp.*	Red, coral, pink, and white	Late spring to summer
◑ Cranesbill, *Geranium sp.*	Rose, lilac, and blue	All summer
● Dutchman's breeches, *Dicentra cucullaria*	White	Mid spring
◑ Foxglove, *Digitalis sp.*	Yellow, white, pink, and purple	Late spring
◑ Goatsbeard, *Aruncus dioicus*	White	Early summer
◑ ● Golden star, *Chrysogonum virginianum*	Yellow	Late spring to summer
◑ Hellebore, *Helleborus sp.*	White, purple, pink, and green	Mid winter to early spring
◑ ● Hosta, *Hosta sp.(pictured below, right and left)*	White to lavender	Summer
◑ ● Jack-in-the-pulpit, *Arisaema triphyllum*	Green with purple, striped	Late spring
◑ Leopard's bane, *Doronicum cordatum*	Yellow	Early to mid spring
◑ ● Lilyturf, *Liriope sp.*	White, blue, and purple	Late summer
◑ ● Lily-of-the-valley, *Convallaria majalis*	White, fragrant	Late spring
◑ ● Lungwort, *Pulmonaria sp.*	Blue, white, or pink	Late spring to early summer
◑ Pink turtlehead, *Chelone sp.*	Pink	Late summer to early fall
◑ Shooting star, *Dodecatheon meadia*	White or pink	Late spring
◑ Snakeroot (Bugbane), *Cimicifuga sp.*	White	Late summer to fall
◑ ● Spiderwort, *Tradescantia sp.*	Pink, white, blue, and purple	Summer
◑ Sweet woodruff, *Galium odoratum*	White	Mid spring
◑ Toad lily, *Tricyrtis hirta*	Purple spotted	Mid fall
◑ Tube clematis, *Clematis heracleifolia*	Blue, fragrant	Mid summer
◑ Yellow corydalis, *Corydalis lutea*	Yellow	Spring to early summer
◑ ● Wake robin, *Trillium grandiflorum*	White	Early spring
◑ Wild ginger, *Asarum sp.*	Purple to brown	Late spring to summer

Shade Preference; partial shade ◑   full shade ●

Tranquil beauty of shade gardens

OCTOBER
Water Gardens

ORNAMENTAL PLANTS FOR THE WATER GARDEN

Fairy moss, *Azolla caroliniana*
Lotus, *Nelumbo sp.*
Papyrus, *Cisperus Papyrus*
Pickerelweed, *Pontederia cordata*
Water canna, *Thalia dealbata*
Water fern, *Ceratopteris pteridoides*
Water hawthorn, *Apogoneton distachyus*
Water hyacinth, *Eichhornia sp.*
Water lettuce, *Pistia Stratiotes*
Waterlily, *Nymphaea spp.*
Water poppy, *Hydrocleys nymphoides*

OXYGENATING PLANTS

Cabomba, *Cabomba caroliniana*
Eel grass, *Vallisneria sp.*
Elodea, *Elodea canadensis*
Sagittaria, *Sagittaria sp.*

PLANTS FOR THE SHALLOW END OR WET BANKS OF THE POND

Arrow arum, *Peltandra virginica*
Blue flag, *Iris versicolor*
Cow lily, *Nuphar sp.*
Giant reed, *Arundo sp.*
Golden club, *Orontium sp.*
Narrow-leaved cattail, *Typha angustifolia*
Pitcher plant, *Sarracenia purpurea (pictured below)*
Sweet flag, *Acorus calamus*
Water clover, *Marsilea sp.*
Yellow flag, *Iris pseudacorus*

Pitcher plants

NOVEMBER
Variegations—Plants of Distinction

VARIEGATED ANNUALS & BIENNIALS
Coleus, *Coleus x hybridus*
Flowering kale, *Brassica oleracea*
Geraniums, *Pelargonium sp.*
Honesty, *Lunaria annua 'Variegata'*
Joseph's coat, *Amaranthus tricolor*
Nasturtium 'Alaska', *Tropaeolum majus 'Alaska'*
New Guinea impatiens, *Impatiens Wallerana*
Ornamental cabbage, *Brassica oleracea*
Snow-on-the-mountain, *Euphorbia marginata*

VARIEGATED BULBS, CORMS, & TUBERS
Caladium, *Caladium sp.*
Canna 'Benegal Tiger', *Canna x generalis 'Benegal Tiger'*
Cyclamen, *Cyclamen hederifolium*
Dog-toothed violet, *Erythronium sp.*
Golden arum lily (yellow calla lily), *Zantedeschia elliotiana*
Tulip, *Tulipa sp., esp. T. greigii, T. kaufmanniana, T. praestans unicum*

VARIEGATED PERENNIALS
Arum, *Arum italicum 'Pictum' and other Arum sp.*
Carpet bugle, *Ajuga reptans*
Coral bells, *Heuchera sp.*
Dead nettle, *Lamium sp. (pictured at right) and Lamiastrum sp.*
Goutweed, *Aegopodium podagraria 'Variegatum'*
Hosta (plantain lily, funkia), *Hosta sp.*
Houttuynia, *Houttuynia cordata 'Chamaeleon'*
Iris, *Iris sp.*
Japanese painted fern, *Athyrium nipponicum 'Pictum'*
Lilyturf, *Liriope muscari 'Variegata'*
Lungwort, *Pulmonaria sp.*
Phormium, *Phormium sp.*
Ornamental grasses, *Carex, Cortaderia, Hakonechloa, Phalaris, etc.*
Sasa, *Sasa veitchii*
Sweet flag, *Acorus calamus 'Variegatus'*

VARIEGATED VINES
Actinidia, *Actinidia kolomikta*
Ivy, *Hedera sp.*
Porcelainberry, *Ampelopsis brevipendunculata 'Elegans'*

VARIEGATED TREES AND SHRUBS
Andromeda, *Pieris japonica cv.*
Butterfly bush, *Buddleia davidii cv.*
Daphne, *Daphne x burkwoodii 'Carol Mackie', D. cneorum 'Variegata'*
Dogwood, *Cornus sp.*
European tricolor beech, *Fagus sylvatica 'Tricolor'*
False cypress, *Chamaecyparis sp.*
Gold dust plant, *Aucuba japonica*
Holly, *Ilex sp.*
Holly osmanthus, *Osmanthus heterophyllus*
Japanese maple, *Acer palmatum*
Weigela, *Weigela sp.*
Yucca, *Yucca sp.*

Arum and dead nettle

DECEMBER
Sounds from the Garden

What disturbs all the subtle sounds of the garden are the sounds of man. Before the advent of power machinery the garden was relatively quiet, even when man was doing his chores. Today, the sounds of a garden are often not tranquil, soothing, and calming. In fact, man has created garden-deafening garden noises. Many of the manmade noises can be described as a form of buzz—but at intolerably loud levels. Walk around any suburban neighborhood, and instead of the quiet, rhythmic push and pull of a handsaw, you hear the roar of a chain saw, the irritating loud whir of a gas-powered string trimmer, and the continuous loud buzzing of power lawnmowers in yard after yard after yard.

The decibel scale measures sound in the same way the Richter scale measures intensity of earthquakes. It is a logarithmic scale. The quietest sound most of us perceive is at about 30 decibels. A sound that is 40 decibels is ten times as loud—50 decibels is a hundred times louder. A gun going off at the side of your head ear ranges between 140 and 170 decibels—which can instantaneously deafen you.

A decibel rating between 80 and 85 (the sound of children on a crowded school bus) is potentially dangerous to human hearing. Such levels of noise are cumulatively damaging. Since there are no home decibel meters, how do you tell if a sound is loud enough to be damaging? If you have to raise your voice to be heard by a person 3 feet away from you, the surrounding noise will hurt you. If you have trouble hearing someone speaking at normal tones 3 feet away when there isn't any ambient noise, your hearing has already been damaged.

Most power garden equipment produces from 80 to 105 decibels. Chain saws top the deafening scale, peaking at 110 decibels. Leaf blowers are also near the top of the chart, not an enviable spot.

What can you about this noise pollution? First, cut down on the power machinery that you use. If you have a small lawn, an old-fashioned reel lawnmower not only makes much less noise, but gives you more exercise. Do you need a chain saw to cut down a small tree with a 2-inch diameter? You can do that, although admittedly slower, with a handsaw.

If you must use power equipment, be choosy in what you buy. Most power equipment does have a decibel rating (often in the fine print). Buy products that have the lowest decibel ratings. Hearing damage is cumulative, so the less time you spend around the din of power machinery, the better. The farther away you are from the sound source, the better. For instance, a backpack blower with the motor near your head that is rated as 100 decibels is going to be more damaging than a vacuum with the same rating whose motor at ground level.

Protect the delicate hearing structures in your years. A wad of cotton in your ear is fairly inefficient, cutting the noise only about 7 decibels. Most earplugs now have a NRR (noise reduction rating) on the package. To work right, earplugs need to be airtight. Foam cylinders can cut noise by 15 to 30 decibels. Plastic earmuffs lined with foam cup tightly around the ears and reduce noise by 15 to 30 decibels. Combine earplugs with earmuffs and you reduce sounds by 25 to 40 decibels. Even though that might put you in a safer zone, remember that the noise you make is polluting—affecting others as well.

We have taken it for granted that hearing loss is a natural part of the aging process. It does not have to be, according to studies in Sudan. Elderly farmers' hearing was tested, and amazingly they had no hearing loss. These farmers, incidentally, never used power machinery, but did everything by hand or plowed using the power of animals. This suggests that the perception of hearing loss as a normal course of aging may simply be a cultural artifact of an industrialized society.

Maiden grass

GARDEN PLANNING

GARDEN PLANNING